MW00809931

Advance praise for *Revolutionizing Feminism*

"Anne Lacsamana shines a bright light on the continuing efforts of local feminists to make nationalist anti-militarist campaigns work for the empowerment of women. If we all take these Filipina activists seriously we'll be able to tally the true costs of the U.S.-led 'global war on terror.'"
—**Cynthia Enloe,** author of
Nimo's War, Emma's War: Making Feminist Sense of the Iraq War

Revolutionizing Feminism

REVOLUTIONIZING FEMINISM

THE PHILIPPINE WOMEN'S MOVEMENT IN THE AGE OF TERROR

Anne E. Lacsamana

Paradigm Publishers

Boulder • London

All rights reserved. No part of the publication may be transmitted or reproduced in any media or form, including electronic, mechanical, photocopy, recording, or informational storage and retrieval systems, without the express written consent of the publisher.

Copyright © 2012 Paradigm Publishers

Published in the United States by Paradigm Publishers, 5589 Arapahoe Avenue, Boulder, CO 80303 USA.

Paradigm Publishers is the trade name of Birkenkamp & Company, LLC, Dean Birkenkamp, President and Publisher.

Library of Congress Cataloging-in-Publication Data

Lacsamana, Anne E.
  Revolutionizing feminism : the Philippine women's movement in the age of terror / Anne E. Lacsamana.
    p. cm.
  Includes bibliographical references and index.
  ISBN 978-1-59451-941-3 (pbk. : alk. paper)
  1. Feminism—Philippines. 2. Women's rights—Philippines. 3. Women foreign workers—Philippines. 4. War on Terrorism, 2001–2009. 5. Philippines—Foreign relations—United States. 6. United States—Foreign relations—Philippines. I. Title.

  HQ1757.L33 2011
  305.4209599—dc22

                                                                                        2011009210

Printed and bound in the United States of America on acid-free paper that meets the standards of the American National Standard for Permanence of Paper for Printed Library Materials.

Designed and Typeset by Straight Creek Bookmakers.

16 15 14 13 12   1 2 3 4 5

*For the victims and families of the extrajudicial killings
and for those who remain disappeared.*

CONTENTS

Acknowledgments

Without the intellectual camaraderie, friendship, guidance, and support of the following individuals and organizations, this book could not have been written.

I am deeply indebted to Delia D. Aguilar and E. San Juan Jr. for instilling in me a critical theoretical lens from which to view the world. Your dedication to social justice and Filipino anti-imperialist feminist struggles has been invaluable for my own personal and scholarly evolution.

In the Philippines, I'd like to thank Judy Taguiwalo, Sarah Raymundo, Roland Tolentino, Elizabeth Eviota, Aida Santos, Princess Nemenzo, Gert Libang, Connie Regaldo, Mila Aguilar, Mayang Taldo, and her late husband, Marcial. Your courage and activism during this period of political repression are an inspiring model for everyone committed to seeing a more peaceful, just world. I'd also like to acknowledge the members of GABRIELA, Migrante International, Migrante-Europe, Samakana-Veterans Chapter, Amihan, Task Force Subic Rape, Freedom from Debt Coalition, Karapatan, and Bayan Muna.

I am grateful for the generous financial support of the American Association of University Women, whose postdoctoral fellowship during the 2008–2009 academic year provided me with the necessary time and resources to write this book.

Several chapters of this book originally appeared in earlier forms in the following publications. Chapter 3 uses sections of my essay "Identities, nation and imperialism: Confronting empire in Filipina-American feminist thought" in *Globalization and Third World Women,* edited by Ligaya Lindio-McGovern and Isidor Wallimann (2009, Ashgate). Chapter 4 expands on earlier ideas presented in my 2004 essay "Sex worker or prostituted woman?: An examination of the sex work debates in feminist theory" in *Women and Globalization,* edited by Delia D. Aguilar and Anne E. Lacsamana (2004, Humanity Books). Chapter 5 appeared in a special issue (Invisible Battlegrounds: Feminist Resistance in the Global Age of War and Imperialism) of Works and Days 59/58 (Volume 29, Nos. 1 & 2, 2010). I am thankful to the editors and publishers of these publications.

I owe special thanks to friends who have sustained me throughout this process with their friendship and laughter: Steve Yao, Kyoko Omori, Chaise LaDousa, Bonnie Urciouli, James Wells, Donald Carter, Heather Merrill, Shelley Haley, Nigel Westmaas, Angel David Nieves, Carl Rubino, Barbara Gold, Amy Gowans, Debra Boutin, Karin Aguilar-San Juan, Michael Viola, and Jeffrey Cabusao.

My colleagues in the Women's Studies Department at Hamilton College, Margaret Gentry and Vivyan Adair, deserve special mention. This book could not have come to fruition without your support and friendship. Thanks for providing me with such a warm and nurturing environment to conduct my research.

I am especially grateful to Jennifer Knerr for seeing the value in this book, Laura Esterman for ensuring a smooth production process, and their colleagues at Paradigm Publishers. It is an honor to work with an independent, progressive publishing house. Many thanks to Jan Kristiansson for her careful attention to detail and excellent copyediting skills.

Without my family, none of this could have been possible. Thanks to my parents, Gayle and Remigio G. Lacsamana, for providing me with a wellspring of unconditional love that has guided me throughout these years.

Finally, words cannot express my gratitude and love for my partner and colleague, Joyce M. Barry. You have read every word of this manuscript without complaint, providing me with incisive and invaluable feedback. This has truly been a collective effort that could not have been achieved without you, Smith, Oscar, Victoria, and Kinsey.

INTRODUCTION

For a people cannot be free, until the women are free.
—*Anonymous, "I Am Woman"*

But our friendship draws
its sustenance
from the rich soil of people's war
It will continue to grow
and bear fruit
for the people.
—*Ma. Lorena Barros, "Two Poems"*

Originating from the anti-imperialist nationalist resistance of the 1960s and 1970s, the multisectoral Philippine women's movement continues the struggle for national sovereignty and women's liberation during one of the darkest periods in recent Philippine history. To date, there have been over 1,100 "extrajudicial" killings of political activists from across the social spectrum (peasants, journalists, lawyers, students, feminists, union leaders, and so on) and hundreds more "disappeared" since the 2001 election of Philippine president Gloria Macapagal-Arroyo. The declaration of the country as the "second front" in the U.S.-led "war on terror" in 2002 has deepened the crisis, with increased militarization occurring throughout urban and rural areas. In addition to targeting the Abu Sayyaf, a bandit group comprising roughly 100 members with alleged loose ties to al-Qaeda and Osama bin Laden, the Arroyo administration has broadened its counterinsurgency operation to include the Communist Party of the Philippines (CPP) and its armed wing, the New People's Army (NPA). As a result, legal activists belonging to civil society organizations affiliated with the Philippine Left have suffered the majority of casualties; despite this, the government had not backed down on its pledge to eradicate the CPP/NPA as of 2010.

Against this backdrop of instability and de facto martial law imposed by the Arroyo administration, I conduct my examination of identity, migration, militarism, and prostitution in the Philippine context. Utilizing a historical materialist analysis, I locate Filipino women squarely within the international division of labor, making explicit the connection between the superexploitation of their labor power at home and their migration abroad to over 197 countries as domestic workers, nurses, nannies, entertainers, and "mail-order brides." This reliance on a historical materialist perspective marks a fundamental methodological and theoretical break from previous postcolonial and/or transnational feminist analyses on the subject. Whereas empirical studies have focused on Filipino women as domestic workers, nurses, or mail-order brides, this book is a comprehensive study of the various factors impacting Filipino women during this period of intensified repression, paying particular attention to the revolutionary collective resistance being waged by members of groups such as GABRIELA (General Assembly Binding Women for Reforms, Integrity, Equality, and Action), Migrante International, Task Force Subic Rape (TFSR), and the Coalition Against Trafficking in Women—Asia Pacific (CATW-AP).

By foregrounding the ideological and political praxis of Filipino women's grassroots organizations, my project illustrates how their radical, anti-imperialist opposition to oppressive forces reveals the limits of and offers alternatives to contemporary academic feminist theorizing that has steadily retreated from progressive analyses of class and class exploitation, the engine driving neoliberal capitalist expansion, in favor of pursuing the cultural or postmodern turn. Within this reigning theoretical purview, attention to structural forms of oppression and collective acts of resistance is replaced with a focus on discursive abstractions, thereby severing analytical accounts from those organizing for social justice outside the academy. In response, this book seeks to reestablish those linkages between knowledge production and existing grassroots movements by examining the durable tradition of Filipino nationalist feminist activism embedded in the popular culture of everyday life.

The incongruities between Western academic feminist thought and the concrete material realities circumscribing the lives of those residing and laboring in a "Third World" formation became apparent during my first visit to the Philippines in 1997. A graduate student at the time, I quickly realized that my training in postmodernist feminist theory failed to equip me with the critical lens necessary to comprehend the totality (a bugaboo in postmodern parlance) of the social, political, and economic conditions characterizing Philippine society. The emphasis Filipino feminist activists placed on understanding the class character of "globalization," and its relationship to gender and sexuality, was directly at odds with the bulk of feminist knowledge production enjoying wide circulation throughout Western academic centers since the mid-1980s. For some scholars, globalization, characterized by the hypermobility of capital, unfettered drive for markets, flexible forms of accumulation, and shifting patterns of production, was thought to usher in a postmodern epoch characterized by fragmentation, disunity, chaos, and multiplicity. As a result, postmodernist practitioners began to view with "incredulity" all appeals to a "grand narrative, such as the dialectics of Spirit, the hermeneutics of meaning, the emancipation of the rational or working subject" (Lyotard 1979, xxiii–xxiv). In short, attention shifted away from structural or "totalizing" concerns to a more localized, antiessentialist "politics of difference" that could be theorized only through discourse and discursive practices.

For the U.S. women's movement, beset by its own exclusionary tendencies, the postmodern retreat from "master narratives" corresponded with the rise of "identity politics" in feminist theory. By the 1980s women of color were denouncing the white solipsism of second-wave feminist writings by calling for greater attention to the diversity of experiences (based on race, ethnicity, class, sexuality, etc.) within the general category "women." These critiques placed women of color at the forefront of destabilizing ideas of shared oppression premised upon essentialist, white hegemonic ideals of womanhood. Discussing this period in feminism's history, Susan Archer Mann and Douglas J. Huffman explain, "The initial challenges to second wave feminism shared a focus on difference, but resulted in two opposing camps: one that embraced identity politics as the key to liberation; and a second that saw freedom in resistance to identity" (2005, 58). The latter camp, of course, refers to postmodernists and their emphasis on the destabilization of self/subject and group identities/categories.

Even though it is clear that the original conception of identity politics in U.S. feminism was incompatible with the deconstructionist trend in postmodernism, largely influenced by the work of French theorists such as Michel Foucault, Jacques Derrida, and Jean-Francois Lyotard, the two modes of analyses began to share significant commonalities. Seyla Benhabib explains that the "theoretical critique of the French 'masters of suspicion' was at the center of *political* critique by lesbian women, women of color, and Third World women of the hegemony of white, western European, or North American heterosexual women in the movement" (1996, 31). Though disagreements ensued over the stability and relevance of individual and group identity, eventually it became clear that "both embrace[d] the view that knowledge is socially constructed and socially situated.... No one view is inherently superior to another and any claim to having a clearer view of truth is simply a metanarrative—a partial perspective that assumed dominance and privilege" (Mann and Huffman 2005, 65). What resulted, then, was a call for "polyvocality and more localized mini-narratives to give voice to the multiple realities that arise from diverse social locations" (Mann and Huffman 2005, 65). In a recent assessment of the discipline of women's studies, Elizabeth Lapovsky Kennedy and Agatha Beins explain that postmodernism "became as important a theoretical approach as historical materialism had been in earlier years" (2005, 5). Indeed, a large number of feminist academicians considered postmodernism to have a "freeing effect, offering new ways of thinking about the complexity of subjectivity, identity, and experience" (2005, 5). Despite its supposedly liberatory and transformative features, however, the postmodern feminist focus on identity and difference has led to a dilemma: How does one formulate a cogent analysis of social inequality amid a sea of multiple, competing, overlapping differences? Or as Joanne Naiman asks, "If, for example, each category of oppression creates a different experiential reality ... what is it that can bring them together? What is the goal they share in common? When does similarity supersede difference or vice versa?" (1996, 13). Reconciling such contradictions is futile, precisely because it would require a "totalizing" frame that contemporary feminist analyses reject. For some critics, including myself, this flattening of differences and the shift in theoretical priorities have led to the depoliticization of the movement, rendering it inutile to confront the neoliberal forces now governing our world order.

A recently published anthology on Filipina-American feminism, referred to as "peminism" by its practitioners, provides a glimpse into some of the limitations of identity-based examinations. With its singular focus on the "hybrid Filipina American experience," *Pinay Power* (de Jesus 2005, 6) is representative of the current brand of theorizing that serves to mask relations of power by substituting a celebratory brand of identity politics in place of a radical historical materialist critique of global capitalism—the lifeblood that sustains the imperial project. Although words such as "imperialism" and "capitalism" are liberally dispersed throughout the various chapters making up the collection, their explanatory potential is occluded by more cultural efforts seeking to "carve out a distinctive space for the hybrid Filipina American experience" (2005, 6). For example, Melinda de Jesus argues that the "legacy" and "ghosts" of U.S. imperialism in the Philippines "haunt" Filipina Americans, resulting in the persistent experience of "alienation, invisibility, [and] trauma" that can be remedied through individual acts of "healing, and resistance" (2005, 6–7). Such opposition, however, is confined to language, exemplified by the deployment of peminism, which "signifies the assertion of a specifically Filipina American subjectivity, one that radically repudiates white feminist hegemony as it incorporates the Filipino American oppositional politics inscribed by choosing the term *Pilipino* over *Filipino*" (2005, 5). Aside from the fact that the 1987 Philippine Constitution declared the national language of the country to be "*F*ilipino" to be inclusive of other vernaculars (which do have the *F* sound) besides Tagalog, the decision to make the switch from *f* to *p* could be purely for the discursive, exotic, and performative potential such words evoke. However, making such a linguistic substitution in no way destabilizes, displaces, or transgresses U.S. hegemonic rule of the Philippines, nor does it effectively challenge or "repudiate" the institutionalized racism of the feminist movement. In short, even though the *structure* of the words might change (peminism/feminism), the *essence* of imperialism, white racism, and U.S. power remain intact (Lacsamana 2009, 77).

At a recent Filipino American conference, keynote speaker E. San Juan Jr. addressed, among other things, the contemporary struggles in the Philippines, the importance of history in comprehending the totality of the current situation, and the role Filipino Americans can actively play toward grasping the complex processes and contradictions that define our reality (Lacsamana 2009, 77). When comparing the politicization process that occurred among the previous generation (those who came to political consciousness during the 1960s–1970s) with that of today's young Filipino Americans, San Juan observed, "We no longer have the 'Manongs' as examples for young Fil-Ams to learn from. In fact, few young Fil-Ams now read Bulosan's writings, much less the biography of Ka Philip Vera Cruz. We have 'model minority' Filipinos like General Taguba, the White House cook, Lea Salonga, celebrities in TV and other media casinos, etc. What else is new? You belong to a new generation in which the ideal of becoming the model 'multicultural American,' while a ruse for suppressing critical impulses, seems to have become obligatory" (2007, 2).

Most important for our understanding of these generational differences is the "disappearance of a radical socialist alternative" (2007, 3) that occurred during the neoconservative climate of the 1980s and continues into the present day. Accompanying this retreat from progressive politics is the ideological shift away from perspectives that emphasize the materiality of social relations (Marxism) in favor of the cultural realm. For San Juan, a convergence of events, in the realms of politics and ideology, has led many Fil-Ams down a directionless and muddled path, fueled in large part by the influence postmodernist thinking has had on contemporary Filipino scholarship, which emphasizes "'success,' or 'agency' [coupled with] readings about the excess of 'spectral presences' of Overseas Filipinos and the 'shamelessness' of the balikbayans" (2007, 1). Similarly, in a perspicacious analysis of Chicano literature and cultural theory, Marcial Gonzalez draws upon the critically acclaimed work of Gloria Anzaldua to highlight the risks involved in embracing the "borderlands" or "mestiza consciousness" (2004, 170) simply for the sake of complexity and ambiguity—a position peminist critical theory appears to advocate. In *Borderlands/La Frontera,* Gloria Anzaldua "exposes the deeply conflicted character of the mestiza psyche" but does not indicate how merely embracing one's dual or fractured identity will necessarily "help change the conditions that cause ideological ambivalence" (2004, 171). Gonzalez compares Anzaldua's analysis of the "mestiza psyche" with Gilles Deleuze and Felix Guattari's concept of "schizoanalysis" (1983), which essentially argues that the state of fragmentation in and of itself is the site of radical potential, irrespective of the structural mechanisms responsible for producing the fragmentation in the first place. Gonzalez contends that this theoretical position "becomes a problem only when the conditions of alienation and social fragmentation are misconstrued as politically progressive or as inherently revolutionary" (2004, 174). There are inherent risks scholars and theoreticians take when they uncritically embrace a postmodern politics of identity severed from the materiality of daily life. For one, this type of theorizing is capable of promulgating the idea that institutionalized forms of oppression can be remedied through the "agency" of individual, autonomous subjects. On another level, it teaches oppressed and dispossessed citizens to merely "'cope' with alienation rather than figuring out ways of overcoming alienation" (2004, 175). Coping, rather than transforming deep structures of oppression, works in favor of the dominant classes, which utilize their positions of power and influence to perpetuate the wholesale deprivation of people based on gender, race, class, ethnicity, nation, sexual orientation, and so on.

In *Ludic Feminism and After,* Teresa Ebert offers one of the first thorough critiques of feminism's preoccupation with postmodernism, explaining that its focus on "linguistic play … substitutes a politics of representation for radical social transformation" (1996, 3). Now that feminism and the "post" theories (poststructuralism, postmodernism, postcolonialism, post-Marxism, etc.) have become synonymous in the West, particularly in the United States, they are endowed with an "inordinate institutional influence in determining which knowledges will be central and which will be marginalized" (1996, 23). Given academic feminism's aversion to modernist discourses and its subsequent elision of the political economy, it is not surprising that "revolutionary knowledges, especially Marxism," are excised from the field (1996, 23). Barbara Epstein echoes similar concerns in her 2001 essay "What Happened to the Women's Movement?" Lamenting that there is no longer a "mass women's movement" in the United States, Epstein explains that "feminist theory, once provocative and freewheeling, has lost concern with the conditions of women's lives and has become pretentious and tired" (2001, 2). For her, the disappearance of the women's movement is related to the overall decline in the

U.S. Left created by a "widespread acceptance that there is no alternative to capitalism" and to feminism's institutionalization in the academy, which has led many theorists to become enamored with the "pursuit of status, prestige, and stardom," thereby turning "feminist and progressive values on their head" (2001, 6, 10). Likewise, Martha Nussbaum argues that the professionalization of feminism has led to an ineffectual movement that "instructs its members that there is little room for large-scale social change, and maybe no room at all.... All that we can hope to do is find spaces within the structures of power in which to parody them, to poke fun at them, to transgress them in speech" (1999, 2). Although the apparent limitations of this particular analytical paradigm should be readily apparent, its defenders dismiss such criticisms, characterizing them as "apocalyptic," chastising detractors for finding "political failure in academic feminism's institutional success" (Wiegman 2005, 41). At the risk of contributing further to the "apocalyptic narration" Robyn Wiegman describes, I maintain that the ascendancy of postmodernism and its variants in the humanities and social sciences, particularly women's studies, has severely hampered feminist theory's ability to confront capitalist processes, the very forces responsible for the production and maintenance of "difference" that is routinely analyzed, deconstructed, and celebrated in current analytical accounts. Thus, one could argue that in its current incarnation, academic feminism has become complicit, rather than oppositional, to the rapaciousness of neoliberal capitalist expansion.

The crisis in capitalism, evidenced by the recent international financial collapse, provides us with an important opportunity to intervene and disrupt the hegemony of ludic knowledge production. The world today, marked by growing inequality within and among nation-states, intensified militarization, and environmental degradation, among other factors, can best be understood through a historical materialist lens. Grounded in the social relations of production, historical materialism makes clear that the oppression of various groups located in the global North and South "cannot be separated from the conditions producing individuals: not just the discursive and ideological conditions but most important the *material* conditions ... that shape discourses and ideologies" (Ebert 1996, 37). The necessity of a radical, socialist feminist perspective focused on the fundamental transformation of global capitalist processes was made abundantly clear to me during research trips to the Philippines. Traveling the streets of Manila, where squatter communities and megamalls collide, where garbage heaps masquerading as mountains transform the urban landscape into an excess of capitalist waste fit only for the most dispossessed to scale, where gated communities flaunt the supposed success of an export-oriented economy, I could not help but notice the contradictions, ruptures, and disjunctures of living in a neocolonial society. Out of a population of 92 million, more than 27 percent, or 23 million Filipinos, live below the Asia Pacific poverty line of $1.35 per day (Dumlao 2008, 1). The current capitalist meltdown threatens to exacerbate the situation as remittances from overseas Filipino workers (OFWs), the mainstay of the Philippine economy, threaten to dry up as thousands of migrants are repatriated back to the country, where unemployment levels have reached an all-time historic high, leaving approximately 4.3 million Filipinos without a job (IBON 2010). As the situation worsens, it will be women and children that bear the brunt of the economic shock, as access to food, water, health care, education, and other basic necessities are scaled back. The Philippines, similar to other Third World countries, exemplifies the failures of over two decades of neoliberal economic globalization policies. Austerity measures mandated by the International Monetary Fund (IMF) and the World Bank (WB) have resulted in a $54 billion external debt burden (Freedom from Debt Coalition 2007), compounded by unfettered "free-trade" policies that have transformed the nation into a haven of cheap, flexible (feminized) labor for transnational corporations.

In a prescient analysis of globalization, Michel Chossudovsky writes that "this worldwide crisis is more devastating than the Great Depression of the 1930s. It has far-reaching geo-political implications; economic dislocation has also been accompanied by the outbreak of regional wars, the fracturing of national societies, and, in some cases, the destruction of entire countries. By far, this is the most serious economic crisis in modern history" (2003, 1). This perspective on globalization stands in sharp contrast to certain feminist analyses of the phenomena, such as those produced by the academic duo J. K. Gibson-Graham. In *The End of Capitalism (as We Knew It)*, they assert that the "death script" of globalizing discourses obscures the more dynamic and complex outcomes of global capitalist processes for some Third World women. Specifically, they claim that "women's involvement in capitalist exploitation has freed them from aspects of the exploitation associated with their household class positions and has given them a view from which to struggle with and redefine traditional gender roles" (1996, 132). In this culturalist account, Gibson-Graham falsely assume that the transformation of gender relations can be achieved without a simultaneous transformation of the political economy, the material basis responsible for maintaining unequal gender relations in the intimate confines of the home. Comparing the discourse of globalization to a rape narrative, they examine the "penetrating" process of capitalism by highlighting the semiconductor industry in Southeast Asia, which has resulted in local "industrial growth" rather than underdevelopment. Indeed, rather than reading this as a "rape event," Gibson-Graham argue that transnational corporations are responsible for "inducing a pregnancy" in the Third World with unlimited potential (1996, 131). As common as such analyses have become in contemporary feminist theorizing, one hopes that the latest crisis in capitalism will begin to shift the theoretical plane back to more substantive accounts that are materially grounded in the social relations of production.

Against the backdrop of globalization's impending decline, my book intends to challenge these theoretical currents by highlighting the revolutionary actions of the grassroots Philippine women's movement, paying particular attention to its more militant arm. In the process of researching the history of Filipino women's collective resistance, I also came to terms with my own personal genealogy. Similar to other Filipino American mestizas, the daughter of a Filipino father and a white mother, I grew up never feeling truly "American" or "Filipino." During the flight home after my first visit to the country, I realized that the historical amnesia I had experienced as a child was mirrored in academic accounts describing U.S.-Philippine relations. Cleansed from these pages was the history of U.S. intervention in the Philippines beginning with the Philippine-American War (1899–1902) and the massacre of over 1 million Filipinos. It occurred to me that this brutal "pacification" campaign was responsible for the migration of Filipinos, like my father, from their homeland to the United States seeking a "better life" from the chronic poverty, hunger, and unemployment resulting from years of U.S. colonial and neocolonial rule.

In Chapter 1, I situate the contemporary human rights crisis within the historical and unequal confines of U.S.-Philippine relations. The viciousness of this imperial encounter established the groundwork for the passage of a series of iniquitous treaties favoring U.S. interests and ensuring Philippine dependency. The maldevelopment of the Philippines prior to the granting of formal "independence" in 1946 is evidenced by the immiserating poverty and social unrest that characterize present-day Philippine life. By illustrating the deliberate strategies employed by the United States to retain its hegemonic power over its former colony, I counter Michael Hardt and Antonio Negri's central thesis that the era of imperialism, specifically U.S. imperialism, has been displaced by a deterritorialized entity known as "Empire" (2000). In addition to highlighting the role of imperialism, this chapter examines recently published works on Philippine historiography. Influenced by "the cultural turn," these texts, I maintain, downplay the importance of U.S. neocolonial domination in favor of focusing on more cultural elements such as gender and race to explain U.S. conquest of the Philippines. By delinking gender and/or race from the political economy in these analyses, the root causes of U.S. imperialism are once more obscured in academic accounts.

Chapter 2 highlights both the history and the collective resistance being waged by members of the Philippine multisectoral nationalist feminist movement. My examination of these various feminist organizations explores the contested relationship between "feminism" and "nationalism" in Western feminist theoretical accounts, arguing that in a Third World neocolonized formation such as the Philippines, women's liberation is a desideratum for national liberation. To adequately understand why members of the nationalist feminist movement are experiencing increased harassment and intimidation requires a broad historical understanding of its origins and affiliations with the anti-imperialist nationalist movement. In contrast to those analytical formulations that dismiss nationalism because of its modernist and patriarchal moorings, this chapter explores the tensions and vigorous debates that occurred between feminists and nationalists during the late 1970s and 1980s to strengthen a revolutionary nationalist brand of feminism that continues to inform the theory and praxis of the movement today. Ultimately, I conclude the Philippine women's movement can serve as a twenty-first-century model for revitalizing a materialist feminism within an international setting, one anchored, moreover, to the new reality of global capitalism.

Tracing the Philippine labor export program (LEP) to the U.S.-backed Marcos dictatorship, Chapter 3 examines how the labor-intensive work of Filipino women migrants has enabled the Philippine government to service its external debt of $54 billion. The result of this ill-informed "development" strategy is 3,400 Filipinos leaving the country each day, with 6 to 8 returning in coffins. The recent international financial collapse, however, poses formidable challenges for the Philippine government as remittances from the approximately 8 million (70 percent women) OFWs decline amid widespread layoffs in numerous "host" countries. This chapter argues that for a nation entirely dependent on an export-oriented economy, the global economic downturn highlights both the schisms in neoliberal development schemes and the limitations in contemporary analytical accounts of Filipino migration. As an alternative to the latter's preoccupation with individual acts of agency and resistance, Chapter 3 contends that the history of collective resistance embodied by feminist grassroots migrant rights organizations is better suited to confronting the contemporary crisis in Filipino labor migration.

Another feature of the Marcos period included developing "tourism" as a mechanism to generate foreign exchange. In addition to overseeing the construction of luxury hotels and cultural centers to attract potential investors, the Marcos administration often relied on the "beauty" of Filipinas to encourage travelers to visit the country. As a result, many young women became "entertainers" and "hostesses" (euphemisms for prostitutes) during this period. Chapter 4 examines the history of prostitution in the country, specifically focusing on recent feminist debates regarding the issue of trafficking versus sex work in the so-called Third World. Over the past several years, many feminist theoreticians have adopted the postmodern-inspired theoretical position of sex work to emphasize the choice and agency of the individual women involved. In contrast, the majority of Filipino feminists insist on using the term "prostituted women" to connote the lack of choice and economic opportunities propelling many young women into the industry. By placing the sexual exploitation of Filipino women within the broader history of U.S.-Philippine relations, particularly U.S. militarism, members of the Philippine women's movement offer a materialist analysis of the traffic in women, thus underscoring the conceptual divide between contemporary knowledge production and grassroots feminist organizing on the subject of Third World prostitution.

Chapter 5 examines the Subic rape case in the context of the U.S.-led war on terror. The December 4, 2006, conviction of Lance Corporal

Daniel Smith for the rape of a twenty-two-year-old Filipino woman (his three codefendants were acquitted for lack of evidence) on November 1, 2005, marked the first time a member of the U.S. military had been tried and convicted on Philippine soil. Remanded to the Makati City Jail to serve a forty-year jail term, Smith was secretly transferred to the U.S. Embassy on December 29, 2006, to await his appeal. Although some writers might suggest a similarity between the Subic rape case and a host of others that have occurred in Okinawa and South Korea, this chapter demonstrates why U.S. neocolonial domination of the Philippines differentiates this situation from other instances of militarized violence. By directly assailing U.S. militarism, and by extension U.S. imperialism, the efforts of Filipino feminist activism underscore the importance of nationalism in a Third World formation.

Chapter One

⟶⟶⟶

STATE OF EMERGENCY

Contemporary Crisis, Historical Roots

Fear history, for no secret can be hidden from it.
—*Gregoria de Jesus*

For U.S. president George W. Bush and Philippine president Gloria Macapagal-Arroyo, these words of warning issued by Filipina revolutionary Gregoria de Jesus rang true on March 25, 2007, when members of the Permanent People's Tribunal (PPT) Second Session on the Philippines found both leaders guilty of "gross and systemic violation of human rights, economic plunder, and transgression of Filipino people's sovereignty" (www.philippinetribunal.org). A symbolic victory for anti-imperialist forces, the tribunal's verdict was a response to the growing lawlessness and corruption that have come to typify contemporary Philippine life since the election of Macapagal-Arroyo in 2001 and the declaration of the country as the second front in the U.S.-led war on terror in 2002. To date, there have been over 1,100 extrajudicial killings and more than 200 forced disappearances of progressive activists during Arroyo's tenure. In their verdict, members of the tribunal highlighted the dismal historical record between the United States and the Philippines, indicting

15

the iniquitous relationship between colonizer and colonized. This latest consensus is similar to the one reached in 1980 when the tribunal convened for the First Session on the Philippines and an international panel of experts "condemned the dominant economic and political role of the United States of America in Philippines and in the region, through the implementation of an imperialist policy" (PPT 2007, 5). By highlighting both the history of U.S. interventionism in the Philippines and the collective Filipino resistance such aggression has generated, the PPT's verdict stands in sharp contrast to prevailing academic accounts that have either declared the death of imperialism or dismissed the class character of the imperial project in favor of more cultural accounts of U.S.-Philippine relations.

The pronouncement by Michael Hardt and Antonio Negri in their widely acclaimed tome *Empire* that "imperialism is over" and that the "United States does not, and indeed no nation-state can today, form the center of an imperialist project" (2000, xiii–xiv) must have come as a surprise to Filipinos who have lived as U.S. neocolonial subjects since being granted "independence" in 1946. Since the September 11, 2001, attacks on the World Trade Center and the Pentagon and the inclusion of the Philippines in U.S. antiterrorism activities, U.S. militarization of the country has intensified. The Defense Department of the United States and the Department of National Defense of the Republic of the Philippines entered into the Mutual Logistics Support Agreement in 2002 and the Security Engagement Board in 2006, resulting in the deployment of thousands of U.S. soldiers as part of a countrywide "antiterror" campaign against the Abu Sayyaf.

This campaign, otherwise known as Oplan Bantay Laya (Operation Freedom Watch), has extended its reach beyond the Abu Sayyaf to include any person or organization designated a "terrorist" by the state, irrespective of its legal status. U.S. secretary of state Colin Powell justified these expansionary powers of government surveillance and aggression by the Armed Forces of the Philippines (AFP) and the U.S. military against members of the Philippine Left in this declaration on August 9, 2002: "The CPP, a Maoist group, was founded in 1969 with the aim of overthrowing the Philippine government through guerilla warfare. The CPP's military wing, the New People's Army, strongly opposes any U.S. military presence in the Philippines and has killed U.S.

citizens there. The group has also killed, injured, or kidnapped numerous Philippine citizens, including government officials" (San Juan 2005, 1). The designation by the United States of the CPP and NPA as "terrorists" emboldened the Arroyo regime to commit widespread human rights abuses against progressive activists. As part of the indictment against the Arroyo and Bush administrations, members of the PPT cited a July 21, 2006, article by *Philippine Daily Inquirer* reporter Armando Doronilla in which he explained:

> The blueprint of war outlined in the "orders of battle" of Oplan Bantay Laya envisages decimation of non-military segments of the communist movement. It is therefore a sinister plan for civilian butchery, a strategy which exposes the military and police to fewer risks and casualties than they would face in armed fighting with the communist guerillas. The emphasis of this strategy on "neutralizing" front/legal organizations helps explain why most of the victims of the past five years have been non-combatants and defenseless members of the left. (PPT 2007, 11–12)

The U.S. training and support of the AFP in its counterinsurgency operations are made possible by members of the "Pentagon and Central Intelligence Agency, [which have] been involved in the conceptualization, planning, [and] training of AFP personnel" (2007, 11). To suggest the end of imperialism, or deny the continuing relevance of the United States in governing world affairs, requires ignoring overwhelming evidence to the contrary. Indeed, if the crisis in the Philippines is any indication, Hardt and Negri's thesis that imperialism has transitioned to a "decentered and deterritorializing apparatus of rule" (2000, xii) known as "empire" is untenable in light of contemporary realities.

In addition to the human rights crisis, Arroyo's tenure was marred by widespread corruption and electoral fraud since her ascension to power following the ouster of President Joseph Estrada by a second "people power" revolution (commonly known as EDSA II). Audio recordings released in 2005 by the intelligence branch of the AFP reveal Arroyo rigging the vote with former elections commissioner Virgilio Garcillano in the now infamous "Hello, Garci" scandal. The tapes reveal Arroyo and Garcillano plotting to manipulate vote tallies by 1 million to ensure her victory over Fernando Poe Jr. In the May 2007 midterm national elections, incidences of intimidation, military-sponsored violence, and "vote-buying" were rampant throughout the country. Eyewitness accounts from delegates of the People's International Observers' Mission, a coalition of twenty-seven participants from twelve countries dispatched to observe the elections, concluded that there was "an intimate relationship between systemic violations of the electoral process in 2007, the ongoing socio-economic crisis in the Philippines rooted in neo-liberal economic policies and the terror of systemic extra-judicial killings" (People's International Observers' Mission 2007, 1). Six months later, a group of dissenting generals staged their second revolt in four years at the Peninsula Hotel in Manila, where they once again decried the legitimacy of the Arroyo administration. Although retaliation against the generals and their supporters was swift and ruthless, their publicized denunciation of the Arroyo regime resonates with some of the most recent international assessments of the country's progress. In June 2008 the World Bank released its annual "World Governance Indicators," which highlighted the Philippines as "having the worst corruption incidence among East Asia's ten largest economies" (Oliveros 2008). This report came on the heels of a June 2007 editorial in the *Philippine Star* that revealed the country had earned the dubious distinction of being one of the "least peaceful countries in the world, ranking 100th among 121 in the first ever Global Peace Index drawn up by the Economic Intelligence Unit." Given the violence and graft characterizing the Philippines, it is not surprising that the country is also considered to be the "weakest Asian economy after Vietnam and the most vulnerable to rising prices and global economic slowdown" (Oliveros 2008).

To understand this latest phase in Philippine history, the most violent and unstable since the Marcos dictatorship, requires situating it within the historical and unequal context of U.S.-Philippine relations. The current transformation of the country into a virtual killing field by the Arroyo administration's nine-year reign of impunity is intimately connected to the brutal "pacification" campaign waged by the United States during the oft-forgotten Philippine-American War (1899–1902). In what is considered to be the "first Vietnam," the United States flexed its imperial strength using a variety of murderous tactics to quell Filipino revolutionary forces. As a result, over 1 million Filipinos were killed by U.S. troops in a depopulation campaign meant to leave nothing but a "howling wilderness" in its wake.

Commenting on the viciousness of this war, historian Howard Zinn explains that "American firepower was overwhelmingly superior to anything the Filipino rebels could put together. Dead Filipinos were piled so high that the Americans used their bodies for breastworks" (1980, 309). So complete was the devastation that Mark Twain, an outspoken critic of U.S. involvement in the Philippines, lamented, "We have pacified some thousands of the islanders and buried them; destroyed their fields; burned their villages, and turned their widows and orphans out of doors; furnished heartbreak by exile to some dozens of disagreeable patriots; subjugated the remaining ten million by Benevolent Assimilation, which is the pious new name of the musket and so, by the Providences of God—and this phrase is the government's not mine—we are a world power" (quoted in Zinn 1980, 309).

Recently, the barbarism of the Philippine-American War reappeared when news surfaced concerning the illegal use of torture by U.S. troops, specifically waterboarding, in the main theaters of the U.S.-led war on terror: Afghanistan and Iraq. Previously known as the "water cure," the United States first "perfected" this form of torture on Filipino rebels during its colonial subjugation of the country. In 1900 a U.S. soldier described the process whereby soldiers would lay Filipinos "on their backs, a man standing on each hand and foot, then put a round stick in the mouth and pour a pail of water in the mouth and nose, and if they don't give up pour in another pail. They swell up like toads. I'll tell you it is a terrible torture" (Kramer 2008, 1). Twain, among other anti-imperialists, was so disgusted by the use of the water cure that he questioned the logic of government policy: "To make them confess what? Truth? Or lies? How can one know which it is they are telling? For under unendurable pain a man confesses anything that is required of him, true or false, and his evidence is worthless" (Blount 2008, 1). Although 1902 marks the "official" end of the Philippine-American War, armed conflicts between U.S. troops and Filipino citizens continued until 1913.

The traditional historical narrative concerning U.S. involvement in the Philippines has typically pointed to the drive for markets and raw materials as a central reason propelling U.S. colonialists during this period. Senator Alfred J. Beveridge's speech on the Senate floor in 1900 confirms these aspirations: "But if they did not command China, India, the Orient, the whole Pacific for purposes of offense, defense, and trade, the Philippines are so valuable in themselves that we should hold them. The archipelago is a base for the commerce of the East. It is a base for military and naval operations against the only powers with whom conflict is possible" (Schirmer and Shalom 1987, 25–26). Two years earlier, on the eve of the Philippine-American War, Senator Henry Cabot Lodge explained to President William McKinley that "with our protective tariff wall around the Philippine Islands, its ten million inhabitants, as they advance in civilization, would have to buy our goods, and we should have so much additional market for our home manufactures" (Schirmer and Shalom 1987, 21–22). As these comments by some of the principal architects of empire in the Philippines reveal, the imperative for capitalist expansion at the beginning the twentieth century was the primary force driving U.S. annexation of the country.

Recently, however, a number of academic accounts examining U.S.-Philippine history have emerged to challenge this long-held view. In her influential work *Fighting for American Manhood* Kristin Hoganson acknowledges that economic "explanations provide a strong rationale for American policies in the Philippines, but they still leave questions" (1998, 13). In her estimation, capitalist motives by U.S. imperialists fail to answer how they were "able to enact their policies over the impassioned protests of anti-imperialists" and why the United States would "forsake its democratic precepts to fight a war of conquest thousand of miles away" (1998, 13). To answer these questions, Hoganson turns to gender and, more specifically, the fear of male degeneracy among U.S. policymakers at the time. Nevertheless, she cautions against simply "adding" gender to the existing historical record, preferring instead to revise the Filipino-American conflict using "gender as a basic building block" (1998, 14). Returning to some of the most notorious imperialists of the time, Senators Beveridge and Lodge, Hoganson deploys her gender analysis to illustrate that worries over "manliness" trumped economic concerns. She writes that "along with manhood, Beveridge also cared about markets, but to him they were a means to an end and not the end itself. In his estimation, the ultimate purpose of commerce was to build character" (1998, 147). For Lodge, she notes, "manly character was not [his] only motive in the Philippines. He spoke also of the 'great markets of the East' and 'our share of the markets of the world.' But to Lodge, wealth came second to character" (1998, 149). There can be no doubt that gender played a significant role in imperial conquest for both colonizer and colonized. However, to argue, as Hoganson does, that capitalist expansionism was only a mere, secondary concern when compared to preserving the manly character of white men seems difficult to comprehend given the historical and contemporary record of the Philippines.

A different approach to the subject of American "manhood" during this time period can be found in Roxanne Lynn Doty's *Imperial Encounters*. In this highly original work, Doty examines and deconstructs the various representational strategies deployed by U.S. colonialists to justify annexation of the Philippines. By arguing that ideas of American manhood combined with race functioned to create a distinctly American identity that could simultaneously differentiate and connect itself with previous European colonial powers, Doty persuasively illustrates how this U.S. version of "white man" "was itself a discursive construction with no positive content, a construction whose meaning depended on the construction of its 'other.' 'White man' was never absolutely present outside a system of differences" (1996, 48). Deconstructing the discursive practices that constituted American (white) manhood, Doty reveals how differences became naturalized, thus enabling U.S. foreign policy makers to deploy "practices that led to the death of more than a million Filipinos and the subsequent denial of their right to government" (1996, 48). Thus, rather than reducing the entire Philippine-American War to fears over male degeneracy, Doty points to the manner in which gender and race were important strategies used by U.S. imperialists to ensure and justify the social, political, and economic domination of the Philippines.

In this regard, Doty's analysis also stands apart from Paul Kramer's *The Blood of Government*. Similar to Hoganson, Kramer revisits the Philippine-American War and determines that "race" was the fundamental reason behind U.S. imperialism in the Philippines. Differentiating himself from other scholarly assessments that have "emphasized the functionality of race to empire, often as 'colonial discourse,'" Kramer asserts that his new history highlights "race as a dynamic, contextual, contested, and contingent field of power" (2006, 2). By focusing on what he calls "particular imperial indigenisms," Kramer's work departs from the more familiar "colonial discourse" paradigm and its attendant functionalism, which require the "organic expression of a seamless imperial project of military conquest, political control, and economic exploitation [and] its analytic exclusion of colonized peoples whose engagement—in whatever complexes of collaboration, resistance, and mediation—is deemed analytically unnecessary" (2006, 23, 21). In the specific case of U.S. colonialism in the Philippines, Kramer argues that a "novel racial formation" developed between Americans and Filipinos, thereby effectively challenging previous historical narratives that have suggested imperialist discourse was simply the "'export' of U.S. racial idioms" (2006, 5). Drawing from the earlier Spanish division of the Philippines into "Christian" and "non-Christian" populations, the new racial formation, according to Kramer, blurs the line between colonizer and colonized. For example, as part of a collaboration with U.S. officials during the colonial period, Filipino elites would often distance themselves from the "non-Christian" population, signaling to Kramer the emergence of an "internal empire" among Hispanicized Filipinos (2006, 5). The various actions of the elites, whom Kramer labels "nationalist colonialists," reveal the way the "new racial formation was the product of intense contestation and dialogue, a joint American-Filipino venture" (2006, 435). In this rendering of U.S.-Philippine history, the inequality wrought by a brutal dehumanizing imperial regime is erased, replaced by a "mutual imbrication of American and Philippine nation-building across almost four decades of transnational encounters" (2006, 7). By limiting his analyses to the cultural lens of race, Kramer creates an illusion of reciprocity between U.S. colonialists and Filipino elites, going so far as to suggest the latter were equally invested in the colonizing process.

To be sure, Kramer's focus on the development of a new racial formation between members of the Filipino elites and U.S. imperialists is, as alluded to earlier, a deliberate analytical move to highlight the complexity and contingency of race-making in particular historical contexts. In this respect, his work exhibits the standard characteristics of a postmodern, culturalist, revisionist history of U.S.-Philippine relations. This criticism is certainly not intended to discount the wealth of information Kramer provides readers concerning the numerous ways Filipinos were racialized during this period. Rather, this criticism means to demonstrate the very real limitations such analyses inevitably have when they fail to ground their understandings of race and/or gender within the concrete, material context of capitalist processes. Though he details the "policy of attraction" the United States deployed to ensure a compliant, collaborator class among Filipino "elites," Kramer's intent to illustrate their "nationalist-colonialist" aspirations flattens the deep divisions inherent within the asymmetrical relationships that make up imperialist projects. As San Juan states, "In a situation of colonialism, client-patron relationship denotes absence of reciprocity" (2000, 203). Nevertheless, in spite of the overwhelming evidence that points to the dominant role the United States has played and continues to play in the daily life of Philippine affairs, academic accounts continue to revise the historical record to offer more sanitized versions of U.S.-Philippine relations.

Using the events commemorating the fiftieth anniversary of Philippine "independence" as her backdrop in *The Star Entangled Banner,* Sharon Delmendo provides readers with a series of examples to illustrate the ongoing relationship between the two nations. Written shortly after the United States declared an all-out war against terror following 9/11, Delmendo revisits the Philippine-American War to argue that "many of the fraught definitions of nationalism that first emerged during the beginning of the United States' entanglement in the Philippines have reemerged as timely and crucial for articulations of American national identity" (2004, 2). The evolution of U.S. nationalism, according to Delmendo, is intimately connected to the development of Philippine nationalism and vice versa. Unlike studies that have failed to acknowledge how U.S. and Philippine nationalisms have been "more deeply knotted together in a dynamic both more mutually indebted to and repudiating of each other," Delmendo's text seeks to illuminate the way "Filipino and American nationalisms have been most intertwined, even mutually constitutive" (2004, 20) of each other. Reminiscent of Kramer, Delmendo neutralizes the unequal relationship between colonizer and colonized because the "Philippine-American engagement has never been one of simple conquest or resistance successful or not, but one of mutual cultural and ideological entanglement that as yet has not been adequately appreciated" (2004, 20). The so-called mutuality between the two nations is best exemplified for Delmendo when the Philippine and American flags became entangled during the celebration of Philippine "independence."

Drawing on the work of Benedict Anderson's *Imagined Communities* (1983), Delmendo creates her own theoretical model of nationalism based on "identity, values, and the state" to expose Philippine and U.S. "co-created" nationalisms (2004, 14, 16). Analytically, Delmendo's framework for understanding "nationalism" casts the United States and the Philippines in the roles of diplomatic "partners" working in a synergistic relationship based on joint goals and commensurate visions. Erasing the very real differences between U.S. imperialism and Filipino anti-imperialist nationalism (what she describes as "anti-Americanism"), Delmendo cleanses the historical record, neutering the colonialist ambitions of the United States.

Nowhere is this more evident than in her concluding chapter, where she recounts the horrors of Samar when U.S. general Jacob Smith ordered his troops to reduce the island to a "howling wilderness." The Samar campaign, particularly Smith's directive to kill everyone above the age of ten, has been widely referenced by scholars seeking to highlight the brutality of U.S. colonialism. Reexamining the event to produce a more "balanced" version, however, Delmendo points to inaccuracies on both sides of the historical landscape. On the one hand, the alleged attack and dismemberment of the U.S. soldiers making up Company C by Filipino combatants has been exaggerated by American historians. On the other hand, Filipino "anti-American" historians are also to blame for "selectively" focusing on Smith's command to kill Filipino children. Citing "at least two Filipino sources [that] document children's role in the Balangiga attack," Delmendo argues that this should help rationalize "to some extent Smith's belief that children were active Filipino insurrectos" (2004, 177). In what way should this new historical information change our perception of the Philippine-American War? Put differently, what function does Delmendo's retelling of the Samar campaign serve in relation to our overall understanding of U.S.-Philippine relations?

By unearthing the "sedulous selectivity" (2004, 178) of both pro- and anti-American historians, Delmendo seeks to reform the historical narrative of the Philippine-American War, repackaging U.S. aggression as a reasonable (in the case of Samar) response to the ferocity posed by Filipino anti-American military forces. Given the asymmetrical relationships inherent within imperial contexts, is it not understandable that Filipino nationalist forces would defend their sovereignty against an outside aggressor? In fact, it is this type of resistance, waged by Filipinos across the country, that is one of the most remarkable and enduring features of the Philippine-American War. Expressions of Filipino nationalism first emerged during the Spanish colonial era with sporadic uprisings occurring throughout the country. After three hundred years of Spanish colonial subjugation, Filipino nationalist resistance culminated with the Philippine Revolution of 1896 and the subsequent defeat of Spanish forces. The establishment of the first Philippine Republic signaled the beginning of Philippine sovereignty, which was violently snatched away by U.S. colonizers in 1899. Although a combination of superior weaponry and a variety of torture techniques led to the defeat of Filipino revolutionaries, the durable tradition of organized resistance, generated by Spanish and U.S. colonialism, continues to be a defining feature of Philippine life. Indeed, the various social movements now under direct attack by the U.S.-supported Arroyo administration were born out of these early anticolonial struggles. To attempt a comparison between the military tactics of a colonizing power and those of Filipino anti-imperialist forces, as Delmendo does, requires one to conveniently forget that these two countries are bound together in an unequal union.

Though analyses focusing on U.S. imperialism, with particular attention to the political economy, run the risk of being dismissed as outmoded and retrograde among certain scholarly circles, I maintain their necessity in light of the present international order marked by the U.S.-led doctrine of preemptive warfare in a post-9/11 world. The postmodern elision of class, particularly in discussions of colonial encounters, has led to fragmentary versions of U.S.-Philippine history that have transformed an imperialist relationship into one based upon mutuality and reciprocity. Contrary to Delmendo's earlier claim that the United States and the Philippines are more mutually culturally and ideologically "entangled" than previously acknowledged, I argue that most U.S. citizens are woefully unaware of Filipino culture (when compared to Filipinos' "tutelage" in American society), much less the (neo)colonial ties binding the two nations together. Understanding this history is particularly important for the approximately 3 million Filipinos currently residing in the United States. As one of the largest groups making up the "Asian American" category, the existence of Filipino-Americans can be directly traced to these early colonial incursions. The unequal power relations between the two countries were most recently evidenced with the deportation of over 460 Filipinos, some U.S. citizens, shackled with their hands behind their backs, denied access to food or water during their grueling flight "home" shortly after the 9/11 attacks. This example of racial harassment dates back to the early years of the twentieth century when Filipinos, primarily men, migrated to the United States as "cheap labor" to work on sugar plantations in Hawaii, along the West coast as migratory farmworkers, and in Alaskan fisheries.

Unlike the exclusion of Chinese, Japanese, and Korean workers, Filipinos were recruited to the United States as "nationals" because the Philippines was considered a U.S. territory. As nationals, Filipinos existed in a state of in-betweenness, denied the most basic rights afforded to U.S. citizens even as their labor power helped strengthen the capitalist foundations of the country. The experience of Filipinos, along with that of other racialized groups in the United States, illuminates the manner in which capital makes use of other forms of oppression, such as race and gender, to keep the working class divided. As Ellen Meiksins Wood explains, "If capital derives advantages from racism or sexism, it is not because of any structural tendency in capitalism toward racial inequality or gender oppression, but on the contrary because they disguise the structural realities of the capitalist system" (1995, 267). The long hours and dehumanizing working conditions that characterized the life of a Filipino agricultural worker helped spark a militant labor movement, frustrating the efforts of white capitalists to maintain a docile workforce. The establishment of the Filipino Labor Union in the 1930s "represented the emergence of ethnic labor unionism and the entrance of Filipinos in the labor movement in America" (Takaki 1989, 323).

As the U.S. economy continued to buckle under the weight of the Great Depression, racial animosities toward Filipinos grew, resulting in race riots such as one in Watsonville where "four hundred white men attacked a Filipino dance hall." Many Filipinos were beaten and one was shot to death" (1989, 328). For whites, especially members of the white working class, the colonial image of Filipinos representing America's "little brown brothers" was flatly refuted as this interview with a white member of an agricultural association reveals: "He is not our 'little brown brother.' He is no brother at all!—he is not our social equal" (1989, 324). The racial hysteria surrounding Filipino migration eventually culminated in the passage of the Tydings-McDuffie Act in 1934, declaring the Philippines a commonwealth, with official independence to follow within ten years. Though certain policymakers would trumpet this legislation as further proof of America's "benevolence" and "goodwill" toward the

Philippines, the act was a strategic maneuver to reclassify Filipinos as "aliens" and restrict their migration to the United States.

The racism Filipinos encountered in the United States was being replicated in the Philippines as part of the free, English-language-based, countrywide public educational system the United States instituted. The inculcation of a "colonial mentality" was achieved with U.S. textbooks that taught Filipinos to "look up to American heroes, to regard American culture as superior to their own and American society as the model for Philippine society" (Davis 1989, 35). The imposition of U.S.-based education in the Philippines during this time period indicates the absence of reciprocity between the two countries. On July 4, 2008, a little over a century after the first influx of U.S. teachers arrived to the Philippines aboard the *USS Thomas* in 1901, U.S. ambassador Kristie Kenney celebrated "Filipino American Friendship Day" by touring a former "Teachers Camp" in Baguio City. Reflecting the imperious attitude of early U.S. colonizers, Kenney claimed that the "Thomasites [teachers arriving on the Thomas] came at a time when travel was not the norm and they did not only teach Filipinos English ... they taught life skills, as well" (Cabreza 2008). Part of this teaching included instilling a deep sense of racial and cultural inferiority among Filipinos, thereby lessening the nationalist consciousness that served as the seedbed for the Philippine Revolution against Spain. For women, the educational system merely reinforced Spanish-imposed ideologies of domesticity and familialism by encouraging young girls to take "home economics" courses to prepare for their roles as wives and mothers.

Having secured its political and ideological aims over the period of formal colonization, the United States put several crucial economic and military agreements in place that would ensure the transition of the Philippines from colony to neocolony. Two days before the United States granted the Philippines "independence" on July 4, 1946, the Bell Trade Act, or "parity" amendment, was passed by the U.S. Congress officially granting U.S. citizens equal rights with Filipinos involving ownership of utilities and natural resources. This free-trade agreement stipulated that U.S. goods could enter the Philippines duty free, in unlimited quantities, whereas all Philippine products would be subject to stringent quotas. Under nationalist pressure by Filipinos the Laurel-Langley Agreement replaced the Bell Trade Act in 1955, removing some of its more pernicious aspects. Nevertheless, it "extended the protection accorded U.S. capital" by providing U.S. investors with equal access to developing the entire Philippine economy (Schirmer and Shalom 1987, 88, 95). The evidence of these lopsided economic arrangements disputes once more the notion that the United States and the Philippines were involved in a "joint venture." When decisions were originally being made about the parity amendment, "U.S. officials repeatedly stressed that the mission should be composed exclusively of Americans, with no Filipino members" (Doty 1996, 93). In fact, the exclusion of Filipinos from economic decisionmaking was understood among U.S. policymakers: "The State Department doubted that any man of necessary caliber would be prepared to accept assignment on a Joint Mission since any joint report would require compromise on views and recommendations of both participants" (1996, 93). These words by former Secretary of State Dean Acheson make explicit that compromise, reciprocity, or mutuality between the two countries was simply out of the question.

In addition to these free-trade agreements, the United States ensured the maldevelopment of the Philippine economy by adopting the recommendations put forth in the 1946 Dodds Report. According to Filipino economist Alejandro Lichauco, this report encouraged the United States to "develop Japan as the industrial powerhouse in Asia while simultaneously preserving the Philippines as a raw material economy" (2005, 47). The rationale for this plan developed after World War II when the "U.S. government made the fateful decision to utilize Japan as the principal base from which to protect American economic and military power in the Far East" (2005, 48). Although in the 1950s the WB touted the Philippines as having one of the strongest economies in the region as a result of a series of import controls, these were subsequently dismantled by the Decontrol Program of 1962 implemented by former President Diosdado Macapagal under pressure by the IMF and the WB. In keeping with IMF-mandated conditionalities, the devaluation of the peso began in 1962 and has had a catastrophic impact on the Philippine population ever since. Each successive president has followed the neoliberal directive of free-trade import liberalization, thus preventing industrialization of the country.

Today, the effects of these neocolonial economic arrangements are evidenced by the massive hunger and unemployment plaguing the population. The most recent statistics indicate that the country now labors under a $54 billion external debt burden (IBON 2010). Out of a population of 92 million, over 70 percent live at or below the poverty threshold. The human dimensions of this economic crisis are ever present: "hungry mothers selling their babies in Nueva Vizcaya; hungry fathers selling their kidneys in Tondo; hungry farmers in rice rich Nueva Ecija eating field rats; infants of indigent parents dying at the rate of one a day at the pediatric ward of the Philippine General Hospital" (Lichauco 2005, 3). As these stories confirm, women and children are the ones who "pay the heavy price of debt repayment and privatization policies where due to the neglect of the health care system and drastic cuts in public spending, child and maternal mortality has worsened" (PPT 2007, 7).

Having established a stranglehold on the Philippine economy, the United States fortified its neocolonial arrangement by entering into two military agreements with the Philippines in 1947: the Military Bases Agreement and the Military Assistance Agreement. Both agreements permitted the United States to develop a dominant presence in the Philippines. In addition to granting the United States the right to use twenty-three bases throughout the country, Article III of the Military Bases Agreement allowed the United States to "construct, install, maintain, and employ on any base any type of facilities, weapons, substance, device, vessel, or vehicle, on or under ground, in the air or on and under the water that may be requisite or appropriate" (Pomeroy 1992, 164). As a result of these provisions, two major U.S. military bases were constructed after Philippine independence: Clark Air Force Base and Subic Naval Base. The Military Assistance Agreement made the overall training of the AFP the responsibility of the United States. To carry out this training, the agreement established the Joint U.S. Military Advisory Group, which would also be used to "assist the Republic of the Philippines on military and naval matters" (1992, 164). These military arrangements placed the Philippines and its people in a precarious relationship with other countries. For example, when the United States became involved in the Vietnam War and began using Clark Air Force Base extensively to carry out its missions, it placed the Philippines, albeit reluctantly, at odds with Vietnam. Furthermore, when the United States began to assume its crusading anticommunist position during the Cold War, the Philippines was forced to do the same. As a result of these agreements, the Philippines became aligned in all aspects with dominant U.S. interests.

Aside from a profound and devastating effect on the economic and diplomatic development of the Philippines, the presence of U.S. military bases had a major impact on the lives of Filipinos, especially Filipino women. During the Vietnam War, U.S. military men came in droves to Subic Naval Base for "rest and recreation," or "R&R." Over time, prostitution became one of the primary services offered to U.S. military men during their stay at Subic. Elizabeth Eviota explains that between "1964 and 1973, the year of the Vietnam ceasefire, a daily average of 9,000 military personnel were going out to Olongapo on 'liberty' and millions of dollars were spent on R and R business" (1992, 136). The sexist and racist ideology that fueled the "entertainment" business around the military bases is summed up by a slogan on one of the most popular t-shirts sold in Olongapo to U.S. military men: Little Brown Fucking Machines Powered by Rice.

In response to the growing abuses perpetrated by members of the U.S. armed forces, an antibases movement emerged to demand the expulsion of military bases from the country. As a result of these efforts, the Philippine Senate rejected an extension on the leases, resulting in the ouster of both Subic Bay and Clark Airfield in 1992. The removal of the bases represented an important step toward the realization of Philippine sovereignty dating back to the establishment of Andres Bonifacio's republic in 1896. Nationalist aspirations were dashed, however, in 1998 when former President Joseph Estrada signed the Visiting Forces Agreement (VFA) into law, allowing the United States unlimited military access to twenty-two ports throughout the country. Under the guise of "joint" military and training exercises between the two nations, known as Balikatan (shoulder to shoulder), the United States is given a virtual "free pass" to impose its social, political, and military will on its former colony.

The presence of the U.S. military has been a crucial component in the latest U.S.-sponsored counterinsurgency program designed to infiltrate and destroy organizations associated with the Philippine Left under the pretext of combating terrorism. The AFP has drawn both international and domestic censure for its role in the human rights crisis. Prior to the Permanent People's Tribunal, UN special rapporteur Philip Alston released a damaging report indicting the AFP for being "in a state of denial" regarding the extrajudicial killings and disappearances of progressive activists, journalists, lawyers, students, and human rights workers

(2007, 2). Even the government-appointed Melo Commission assailed the military for its actions: "By declaring persons enemies of the state, and in effect, adjudging them guilty of crimes, these persons have arrogated unto themselves the power of the courts and of the executive branch of government. It is as if their judgment is: These people, as enemies of the state, deserve to be slain on sight. This, they cannot do" (Melo Commission Report 2007, 77).

Like previous counterinsurgency operations, the tactics used by the AFP have been particularly onerous for women involved in progressive organizations. For example, reports indicate that government forces have murdered several women from GABRIELA, with women leaders being "stripped naked and molested by military personnel. Sexual violence is used both as a form of torture and to create fear among women" (PPT 2007, 14). This hearkens back to the late 1980s when, during the Aquino administration, the AFP was asked to intensify operations once more against the NPA. Cynthia Enloe writes that the "Philippine army followed a military doctrine that had been fashioned by the American military in the 1980s especially for use by allied governments against dissident forces in Central America" (2000, 125). During this period, rape became the modus operandi for creating fear among the population because the organized activities of Filipino women were perceived as "doubly subversive: not only is she challenging the government to provide adequate services, she is questioning the very sexual divisions of labor on which the current political order rests" (2000, 126). Despite the threats and acts of violence committed against women activists, the Philippine women's movement remains one of the most vital forces in the anti-imperialist nationalist movement. Deploying a two-pronged analysis that links women's liberation to national liberation, Filipino feminists make clear that the latter cannot be achieved without the former.

This connection has been most clearly articulated in the recent protests concerning two high-profile rapes of Filipino women by U.S. military personnel. Rallies and vigils have been organized by members of the women's movement to demand justice for "Hazel," a twenty-two-year-old Filipino woman raped by a U.S. soldier on February 18, 2008, in Okinawa. The plight of "Hazel" is eerily reminiscent of the widely publicized Subic rape case involving the November 1, 2005, rape of a twenty-two-year-old Filipino woman, "Nicole," by a U.S. soldier as three of his friends cheered him on. Although the December 4, 2006, conviction and sentencing of Lance Corporal Daniel Smith to forty years in a Philippine jail by Makati regional trial judge Benjamin Pozon marked the first time a member of the U.S. military had ever been tried, convicted, and sentenced on Philippine soil, this victory would be short-lived: Smith was secretly transferred to the U.S. Embassy on December 29, 2006, to await his appeal. Although I return to this particular case in a subsequent chapter, I highlight these campaigns waged by members of the Philippine women's movement to illustrate the way women's liberation and Philippine sovereignty continue to be circumscribed by a lengthy history of U.S. military intervention dating back to the signing of the Military Bases Agreement on March 14, 1947.

The revolutionary actions of Filipino foremothers Gabriela Silang, Gregoria de Jesus, and Tandang Sora, who bravely fought for Philippine sovereignty in the war against Spain, are echoed in the work of contemporary women activists. Although the Philippines has been internationally recognized as having one of the most vibrant women's movements, its history has received scant documentation. Given the movement's distinct articulation of a nationalist feminism, I contend the Philippine women's movement can serve as a twenty-first-century feminist model for collective, revolutionary resistance against the excesses of U.S. hegemonic rule by recuperating the critical categories of class and imperialism in a post-9/11 world marked by war, growing inequality within and among nation-states, environmental degradation, and so on.

Chapter Two

NOTES ON THE "WOMAN QUESTION"

Nationalist Feminism in the Philippines

> No uprising fails. Each one is a step in the right direction.
> —*Salud Algabre*

These inspiring words by Salud Algabre, a prominent leader in the 1935 *Sakdal* peasant revolts against U.S. imperialism, have particular resonance for contemporary Filipino women carrying on the struggle for national sovereignty and women's liberation during one of the most dangerous and repressive periods in recent Philippine history. Despite international condemnation and censure, the human rights crisis continues with killings and kidnapping of activists by the AFP. Among the disappeared are Ma. Luisa (Luing) Posa Dominado, abducted from Iloilo on April 12, 2007. Having devoted her life to social justice and human rights work, Dominado was one of the founding members of Malayang Kilusan ng Bagong Kabbaihan (MAKIBAKA, or Free Movement of New Women), a women's liberation organization established in 1970. Less than a year before her kidnapping, on June 26, 2006, two students from the University of the Philippines, Sherlyn Cadapan and Karen Empeno, were abducted by soldiers from a farming community in Bulacan. According to the eyewitness testimony of another kidnapping victim, Raymund Manalo, who met the two young women at the military camp where they were being detained, Cadapan explained that she had "experienced heavy torture" and had been raped on multiple occasions (Castaneda 2007, 1). Though Manalo was eventually able to escape his captors, his account of Cadapan and Empeno suggests military officials killed them both in the summer of 2007.

Activists have also been kidnapped, tortured, harassed, and murdered by government agents according to testimony presented at the Permanent People's Tribunal Second Session on the Philippines. On February 28, 2006, Liza Maza, representative of GABRIELA Women's Party (GWP), the political arm of GABRIELA, had to seek refuge in the House of Representatives, along with four other lawmakers, for fear of being arrested on trumped-up charges of "rebellion" put forth by the Arroyo government. Accused of being members of the CPP and the NPA, the lawmakers, collectively known as the Batasan 5, remained in the custody of the House of Representatives until the charges were dropped several months later. Shortly after this incident, on August 5, 2007, immigration officials at Ninoy Aquino International Airport prevented the national chairperson of GABRIELA USA, Professor Annalise Enrile, from boarding her flight home to Los Angeles. Though she never received an adequate explanation from government authorities regarding her detainment, reports surfaced that her name along with those of two of her traveling companions, Judith Mirkinson and Ninotchka Rosca (all U.S. citizens), had been placed on a mysterious government "watch list," which effectively banned them from leaving the country (Mondelo 2007). Referred to as the GABNet 3, they were eventually allowed to return to the United States on August 14, 2007, after their situation garnered international media attention.

Assessing the state of the Philippine women's movement in such perilous times requires a broad historical understanding of its origins and affiliations with the anti-imperialist nationalist movement. Before proceeding to this history, however, I want to make a few preliminary comments regarding the often-contested subject of feminism and nationalism in contemporary postmodern/postcolonial/transnational academic accounts. Although not intended to be a comprehensive overview, what follows is a thematic sketch highlighting the major trends in prevailing cultural criticism. In much of this scholarship, as a result of the cultural turn, it has become de rigueur to reject nationalism and nationalist projects outright because of their relationship to modernity and modernist traditions. Theorists building upon the highly influential work of Edward Said's *Orientalism* (1978) and Benedict Anderson's *Imagined Communities* (1983) evince certain features that are hallmarks of this particular analytical position. For one, contrary to their usual meticulous attention to specificity and multiplicity, most postmodern/postcolonial critics homogenize the colonial experience by emphasizing its cultural components at the expense of economic and political imperatives. In one of the few critiques of this analytical standpoint, Judith Whitehead, Himani Bannerji, and Shahrzad Mojab argue that this tendency results from the postcolonial inclination to interpret "the past four hundred years of European and Third World interaction through a basic cultural opposition between Self and Other, colonizer and colonized" (2001, 5). Even though binary logic is now considered a bugbear in postmodern/postcolonial thinking, the original emphasis on the self/other duality has had a powerful influence on the direction of this brand of theorizing. As a result of this cultural reductionist framework "colonized and ex-colonized peoples often appear to be constituted by the single identity of cultural colonialism rather than the multiple identities which realistically frame their lives and choices" (2001, 6).

In a similar vein, the diversity of "nationalisms" and their application in specific contexts are supplanted by the deployment of a generic "nationalism" that is always considered retrograde in postcolonial and transnational feminist literature because of its modernist and patriarchal moorings. In the critically acclaimed collection *Scattered Hegemonies*, Inderpal Grewal and Caren Kaplan delineate this line of reasoning: "When modernity takes shape as feminism, therefore it collaborates with nationalism. In its nationalist guise, it cannot be oppositional. The need to free feminism from nationalist discourses is clear" (1994, 22). Although Aijaz Ahmad reminds us that "nationalism is no unitary thing" that can be merely conceived at the "level of theoretical abstraction alone" (1992, 7), the "totalizing" definition of nationalism offered by Grewal and Kaplan exemplifies the postcolonial feminist position on the subject.

A variation on this theme can be found in the work of feminist scholars who have criticized the patriarchal tendencies endemic to most nationalist movements. Cynthia Enloe's observation that "nationalism has typically sprung from masculinized memory, masculinized humiliation and masculinized hope" (1990, 44) has become one of the more widely cited and representative examples of this line of thinking. Others, such as Anne McClintock, have attributed the exclusionary characteristics of nationalist movements to the "family trope" whereby gender difference is naturalized within the "family image ... to figure *hierarchy within unity* as an 'organic' element of historical progress, [thus] legitimizing exclusion and hierarchy within non-familial (affiliative) social formations such as nationalism, liberal individualism and imperialism" (1993, 64). Geraldine Heng elaborates on this idea by illustrating how nationalist movements deploy such terms as "motherland," "mother tongue," and "founding fathers" to "hold together the affective conditions, the emotive core, of nationalist ideology and pull a collection of disparate peoples into a self-identified nation" (1997, 31). In doing so, feminists have argued that nationalist ideology reifies women's subordination within the nation, relegating the specific facets of their oppression to the margins. As a result, some feminist theorists have proposed abandoning the nation-state altogether. For example, expanding upon Anderson's definition of the nation as an "imagined political community" (1983, 6), postcolonial feminist thought projects the state as an "unstable fiction whose desire must be continually posed and questioned" (Alarcon, Kaplan, and Moallem 1999, 6). Reducing nations and nationalist struggles to texts that can be read and deconstructed, so the logic goes, frees oppressed groups from the crisis produced by an exclusionary state apparatus that fails to recognize their "difference." This so-called dissolution of the nation-state is predicated upon the discursive displacement of "structuralist typologies" that divide the world between colonizing and colonized countries (metropole/periphery) by a supposedly more fluid vision characterized by borders and boundaries (Alarcon, Kaplan, and Moallem 1999, 4–5).

Not surprisingly, the concepts of imperialism and, by default, national liberation struggles accompany the death of the nation-state in the postcolonial purview. To illustrate, Michael Hardt and Antonio Negri argue that we have entered into a deterritorialized era of "empire" where resistance will be waged across geographic space and time by a nebulous formation called the "multitude" (2000, xi–xv), rather than among progressive forces constituting anticolonial movements. The latter, now considered anachronistic in the current epoch, serve as reminders of the "poisoned gift" (2000, 132) of national liberation struggles. By flattening power differentials between and among nation-states through this linguistic shift, these theories conveniently locate resistance within the liminal spaces "between woman and nation" where hybrid subjectivities are able to flourish outside the disciplinary regulations of modernity.

For those struggling to survive in neocolonized zones, such as the Philippines, the preceding analytical abstractions surely appear out of synch with present-day realities. Life in the interstices is simply not an option for the majority of Filipinos, whose lives have been circumscribed by U.S. neocolonial policy since the granting of formal independence in 1946. Make no mistake; the brutality of this iniquitous arrangement punctuates everyday life, as evidenced by the political killings and forced disappearances currently gripping the nation. Theoretical accounts that perceive national liberation projects as merely "reflections of an expansionary, European cultural identity" effectively obscure the material inequalities wrought by imperialism, thereby casting anti-imperialist nationalist movements as relics of a bygone colonialist era (Whitehead, Bannerji, and Mojab 2001, 11). The pervasiveness of this particular theoretical lens has insinuated itself into almost all corners of the academy, creating a yawning gap between knowledge production in the West and the concrete realities of those living in the global South, like the Philippines, where the desire for national liberation has been a defining feature of the country's historic confrontations against imperial regimes. This history, specifically Filipino women's lengthy involvement in the nationalist movement, must be understood to thoroughly understand why women's liberation is essential for national liberation in a neocolonized Third World formation.

The anti-imperialist brand of Philippine feminism has its roots in the revolutionary actions of women such as Gabriela Silang, Gregoria de Jesus, Teresa Magbanua, and Melchora Aquino (Tandang Sora), to name a few who fought in the war against Spain. In one of the few scholarly assessments of the Philippine women's movement, Leonora C. Angeles explains that it was not "raw feminism" or "pro-women sentiments" that drove these women to "fight the colonizers but their deep sense of patriotism or love of country" (1989, 110). This early articulation of nationalism is evidenced by the following statement issued by Tandang Sora shortly before she was forced into exile for her participation in the war: "I have no regrets and if I've nine lives I would gladly give them up for my beloved country" (San Juan 1998, 154). Though achieving liberation from over three hundred years of Spanish colonial rule was the primary motivation behind certain Filipino women's activities at the time, I concur with Angeles that "transcending the social role limitations imposed upon them as women was proof enough that they had sharply perceived not only the economic and political evils of colonialism but also the sex inequalities engendered by the social order" (Angeles 1989, 110). Their radical politicization was undoubtedly produced by two major developments during Spanish colonial rule: the feudalization of Philippine society through the privatization of public lands and the imposition of Catholicism. Working in tandem, these developments significantly altered the social landscape for men and women and, in the case of the latter, introduced a rigid social code predicated upon morality and motherhood that continues to permeate contemporary Philippine gender ideologies. Given the exclusion of women from most aspects of public life, religion functioned to instill in them an "infinite capacity for forbearance, suffering, and forgiveness of all venial, mortal, and male sins, obscuring in the process their capacity for involvement in things other than hearth, home, and heaven" (Santos 1984, 3–4). It is within this social and historical milieu that the early struggles of Filipina revolutionaries gain their particular significance.

Because the first stirrings of nationalist consciousness among women were generated in direct response to the stultifying conditions created during the Spanish period, it follows that some would become active combatants in the fight against U.S. colonialism during the Philippine-American War (1899–1902). The defeat of the first Philippine republic and the institution of U.S. rule posed new challenges for Filipino women attempting to negotiate another set of foreign occupiers. Though religious teachings continued to wield enormous influence over women's sexuality, it was the intensification and uneven development of capitalist relations and the imposition of the U.S.-based education system that had the most impact on women at the time. In her carefully detailed work, *The Political Economy of Gender*, Elizabeth Eviota argues that the penetration of capitalism into Philippine society led to greater differentiation between men and women's labor power: "Productive and reproductive work became clearly separated and women's independent production was transformed into waged labour at the same time that this production was increasingly undermined.... [Women] were forced to withdraw exclusively to reproductive work" (1992, 64). The sexual division of labor Eviota describes was buttressed by the countrywide educational system, which "took older children, traditionally housekeepers and mother substitutes, from the home, thus limiting, too, the options of mothers to go into productive work" (1992, 75). With this emphasis on domesticity and motherhood, access to education had a significant effect on Filipino women, particularly those from the wealthier and propertied classes.

As was the case with the social purity campaigns launched by their U.S. counterparts in the late nineteenth and early twentieth centuries, newly educated Filipino women from the privileged sectors entered the public sphere to engage in a range of philanthropic initiatives. As a result of these efforts, the Filipina suffrage movement was born in 1906 with the formation of the Asociacion Feminista Ilonga (Association of Ilonga Feminists), followed by the Society for the Advancement of Women in 1912, and culminating in the founding of the National Federation of Women's Clubs in 1921 (Santos 1984, 5–6). It would take several more years of campaigning by Filipina suffragists before they would be formally granted the right to vote in 1937. In her discussion of this period, Santos notes that many historians attribute the success of Filipino women's franchisement to the encouragement and support of U.S. colonial authorities. Raising the possibility that colonial participation in these campaigns was an attempt to divert women's attention away from the growing independence movement, Santos argues that this signals an "indirect, implicit recognition of women's ability to turn the tide" for Philippine national liberation had this been their main focus at the time (1984, 7). This is a compelling rationale for U.S. support of Filipino suffragists and one that seems plausible because their "intellectual bondage to the Americans was so complete and totalizing" that the majority "failed to see the immediate connection between the subordination of women and the subjugation of their nation" (Angeles 1989, 118). Their elite status also prevented many suffragists from developing important connections with other Filipinas, particularly poor women, some of whom worked in their households as caretakers and servants (Eviota 1992, 74).

For working-class and peasant women, membership in trade unions and other progressive groups served as the seedbed for their politicization during the American period. Though more attendant to issues pertaining to class and labor than to the bourgeois politics of the suffrage movement, most of these organizations failed to take women's concerns seriously. Thus, it was not surprising to see women comprising the rank and file in unions while "men were the officials," nor was it unusual to see women assigned gender-specific tasks in their local chapters (1992, 95). These asymmetrical gender relations were also prevalent in anti-imperialist groups, highlighting the ideological schisms between women's liberation and national liberation. Nonetheless, women's participation in underground organizations such as the Hukbo ng Bayan Laban sa Hapon or Hukbalahap (Huk, or People's Army Against the Japanese) movement, which emerged to challenge Japanese occupation of the Philippines during World War II, marks another chapter in the history of Filipino women's involvement in struggles for national self-determination.

Comprised of peasants affiliated with the Socialist Party and the Partido Komunista ng Pilipinas (PKP, or Communist Party of the Philippines), women's involvement in the guerrilla army of the Huks resembled that of their union counterparts, with assigned tasks predictably differentiated along traditional gender lines. Following the war and the eventual merger between the Socialist Party and the PKP, women continued to work as caretakers in the newly organized Hukbong Mapagpalaya ng Bayan (Army of National Liberation), otherwise known as the official military arm of the communist party. According to Lois West, Filipino women's membership in the PKP in the postwar period of the 1950s "marked the beginning of the influence of the Left on the women's liberation movement, and the prioritizing of class issues and nationalism over gender" (West and Kwiatkowski 1997, 151). Nevertheless, despite women's subordinate positions in these organizations, relations between men and women active in the Huk movement improved over time, according to Angeles. Citing interviews with Huk members, she explains that a "more egalitarian division of reproductive domestic labor was observed among men and women in the Huk movement than in ordinary working class families in the lowlands, [with] males encouraged and trained to do the cooking, washing and childcare" (1989, 141). Moreover, in terms of courtship and marriage, there is evidence to suggest that Huk unions were "more enduring and faithful than ordinary bourgeois relationships" (1989, 142). Even so, the overall political ideology informing the PKP and its membership at the time reduced all other facets of oppression to class, thereby preventing it from developing a "comprehensive framework to liberate women from their specific forms of oppression" (1989, 146). This failure to adequately theorize the "woman question" in the early history of the Philippine Left would continue to plague the revolutionary movement well after a rectification campaign led to the eventual dissolution of the PKP and the establishment of the Communist Party of the Philippines in 1968.

The late 1960s was a period characterized by the steady deterioration of social, political, and economic conditions throughout the Philippines, largely stemming from neocolonial arrangements put in place prior to the granting of formal independence in 1946. Iniquitous trade agreements such as the Bell Trade Act, the Laurel-Langley Agreement, and the Dodds Report, coupled with structural adjustment programs mandated by the International Monetary Fund and the World Bank, hastened the development of a national democratic movement consisting of the CPP, the NPA, and the National Democratic Front (NDF). Disillusioned with the strategies utilized by the PKP, the student-led national democratic movement, influenced by the work of Mao Zedong, developed an analytical framework emphasizing the semifeudal character of Philippine society.

The original women's organization to develop from within the contours of the national democratic struggle was MAKIBAKA in 1969. MAKIBAKA's first major protest occurred in 1970 outside the Miss Philippines Beauty Pageant, where members urged Filipino women to "join in the emancipation of women from the feudal restraints which prevent their full participation in the struggle for national democracy" (Angeles 1989, 147). Taken from the group's manifesto, this statement illustrates both MAKIBAKA's commitment to the nationalist movement and its implicit understanding that women's emancipation could be achieved only after the Philippines was liberated from neocolonial bondage.

Although radical in orientation, the organization's analysis of "women's oppression" was symptomatic of the larger national democratic movement as a whole. That is, similar to their comrades in the PKP, MAKIBAKA's members treated women's oppression as merely a symptom of a class-based society. According to Ma. Lorena Barros, the primary spokesperson of the group, "The broad masses of the Filipino people must first be liberated before any sector, such as women, can be liberated.... It is only by her full commitment in the struggle to liberate the broad masses of the Filipinos from foreign and feudal oppression, the struggle for national democracy that the Filipina can prove herself truly the equal of men" (Angeles 1989, 153).

Some have suggested that the limitations of MAKIBAKA's analysis of the woman question can be attributed to the demands necessitated by the historical events of the late 1960s and early 1970s, specifically the Vietnam War and the increasing corruption of the Marcos regime. For example, Aida Santos comments that the urgency to "make the majority of Filipinos aware of the class contradictions existing within Philippine society" took precedence in the national democratic struggle, rendering women's oppression a secondary, less pressing concern (1984, 9). In light of the various atrocities occurring at home and abroad, many members of MAKIBAKA were reluctant to raise the issue of women's subordination for fear that it would be considered "peripheral, or even sectarian" (Angeles 1989, 155). Similar to the position of other Third World revolutionary women's groups at the time, MAKIBAKA's reluctance to simultaneously push for both women's liberation and national liberation stemmed from its aversion and resistance to "feminism" and "feminist" formulations, which it summarily dismissed as "Western" and "bourgeois."

This distinction between feminism and women's liberation is a crucial one to make, as Filipino feminist theorist Delia D. Aguilar explains, "Feminism in revolutionary third world struggles was then anathema. It was considered bourgeois, individualist, and divisive. I understood well that MAKIBAKA ... stood for the liberation of women, not feminism" (Aguilar and Aguilar-San Juan 2005, 171). After the declaration of martial law in 1972, MAKIBAKA was driven underground, an example of how the "militant sections of the women's movement became an integral part of the anti-imperialist, anti-feudal, anti-capitalist, and anti-fascist movement advocating for the end of the U.S.-supported Marcos dictatorship" (Santiago 1995, 121). Reflecting on the role of women's participation in the struggle, Barros remarks, "If an armed conflict does arise, we will fight alongside the men. We should take up arms if necessary. We are working for a better society for men and women alike, so why should men always bear the brunt of struggle?" (quoted in San Juan 1998, 161). The revolutionary life of Lorena Barros was cut short in 1976 when, during an encounter, government agents gunned her down.

Throughout this period of intense repression, the woman question continued to be debated among Philippine nationalists with the "reaction of men in and outside the struggle [ranging] from ridicule to dismissal" (Eviota 1992, 96). Aguilar, one of the primary authorities on the subject of the nationalist feminist movement, describes her feelings at this particular historical moment: "I was determined to engage the 'woman question' among my revolutionary comrades because, by this point, the limitations of the national democratic platform's stance on women had become apparent to me. The fights I had were angry, fierce, and heated.... I questioned what I saw then as the productivist orientation of the movement and its instrumental reckoning of women's participation in it. I wanted conventional gender relations addressed and changed" (Aguilar and Aguilar-San Juan 2005, 171–172).

In letters and essays published throughout the 1970s and into the early 1980s, Aguilar questioned the stubborn, orthodox view among members of the Philippine Left that maintained women's equality was "secondary" in the anti-imperialist struggle. Her research on how traditional gender ideologies informed both the public and private spheres, with particular attention to the reproductive labor women perform at home, resulted in the breakthrough 1988 publication of *The Feminist Challenge*.

Applying the critique that Western Marxist feminists had launched against the crude economism of traditional Marxism to the situation in the Philippines, Aguilar commented, "Just as some Marxist feminists err in giving primacy to ideology in order to call attention to the oppression of women, we have in the main paid little heed to the ideological constructs that both reflect and intensify the concrete conditions of women's subjugation" (1981, 173). Unfortunately, the insistence that women's equality would emerge once national liberation was achieved prompted her to explain that such a distorted understanding of women's oppression "flies in the face of the experience of existing socialist countries where, despite the very real gains won by women, their subordination persists" (1981, 175). In a semifeudal country where traditional gender relations had been determined by the Catholic church during the Spanish period and then further reified with U.S. colonization, understanding the specific nature of women's oppression was necessary, if not unsettling, to

Filipinos who had grown accustomed to a "female object who [had] been taught to delight in servitude while modestly claiming the 'power behind the throne,' and a male subject whose self-image [derived] from a certain degree of authority at home" (1981, 174).

During this time, it was also not uncommon for Filipino women advocating for the serious treatment of women's oppression to be labeled "divisive." Nonetheless, "throughout the rest of the dictatorial regime, women's groups within or outside the National Democratic Front, including women's religious groups, were engaged in pressure politics" (Eviota 1992, 96). Following the lifting of martial law in 1981 and the assassination of Senator Benigno "Ninoy" Aquino Jr. in 1983, a time many Filipino activists refer to as the opening up of a "democratic space," women's organizations such as Kalayaan (Katipunan ng Kababaihan Para sa Kalayaan, or Women's Collective for Freedom), PILIPINA (Kilusan ng Kababaihang Pilipina, or Movement of Filipino Women), NOW (National Organization of Women), KABAPA (Katipunan ng Bagong Pilipina, or Collective of New Filipinas), SAMAKANA (United Urban Poor Women), AWARE (Alliance of Women for Action and Reconciliation), and WOMB (Women for the Ouster of Marcos and Boycott) began to flourish (West and Kwiatkowski 1997, 154). Diverse in their political affiliations, these groups helped form the backbone of an emerging women's movement in the Philippines. While some, like AWARE and WOMB, initially organized to protest the Marcos dictatorship, organizations like Kalayaan, PILIPINA, and the Center for Women's Resources (CWR) had closer leanings toward the national democratic movement and were therefore more committed to analyzing the woman question in Philippine Left politics (Angeles 1989, 182–188). More importantly, Kalayaan and PILIPINA were among the first women's groups to publicly adopt the term "feminist," arguing "there can never be genuine social transformation unless women are liberated from their specific forms of oppression as women" (Angeles 1989, 185). In 1984 a coalition of women from Kalayaan, PILIPINA, and CWR came together to establish GABRIELA, now considered the largest federation of women's groups in the country, with over two hundred member organizations. Similar to women in Kalayaan and PILIPINA, members of GABRIELA also began calling themselves "feminists," making "sure to explain that they were appropriating the label for themselves and imbuing it with their own nationalist content" (Aguilar and Aguilar-San Juan 2005, 173). Undoubtedly, the early years of the 1980s proved to be a watershed moment for the nascent Philippine women's movement.

For the remainder of the decade, however, a series of important events occurred that threatened the overall progress of the women's liberation struggle. For one, the snap presidential elections of February 1986 endangered the cohesiveness of the various women's groups involved under the broad umbrella coalition of GABRIELA, exposing a fault line between those that were more closely affiliated with the revolutionary national democratic movement and those that were not. Specifically, with the potential election of Corazon Aquino, the Philippines' first woman president, the women's movement became divided over whether or not to support or boycott the election (Angeles 1989, 193). The decision to boycott among certain grassroots women's organizations, particularly those representing the peasantry and the urban poor, resulted in what has been described as a "middle-class fall-out" from GABRIELA, with the remaining groups in the coalition aligning themselves with the national democratic struggle (1989, 194). In the end, the Aquino administration did not prove to be a women-friendly administration. Lilia Santiago explains that the alliance between certain sectors of the women's movement and Aquino "eroded" because of three main policy decisions: political repression of progressive activists, thus subjecting women to a "brutal and more devious form of militarization"; her failure to implement genuine land reform, which led to the "greater marginalization of women and peasant farm workers"; and her close ties to the Catholic church, which severely undermined progress in the critical area of women's reproductive health (Santiago 1995, 124). Despite the political divisions and disagreements among certain women's organizations at the time, the Philippine women's movement remained vibrant, as groups inside and outside the purview of GABRIELA worked on a number of important issues related to improving the overall status of Filipino women.

The democratic space during the post-Marcos period also helped usher in a new phase in Philippine politics, with a number of foreign governments and grant agencies offering financial assistance to both governmental and nongovernmental organizations (NGOs). Given the breadth and scope of its organizing, the Philippine women's movement attracted the attention of foreign donors interested in promoting gender and development schemes. By the early 1990s, the fruits of these efforts were evident in the increase of women's official "desks" and committees, leading some to fear grassroots activism had been co-opted and contained by the growing "NGOization" of the movement (Aguilar 1997, 313). Although securing funding has long been a critical source of support for women's movements throughout the world, reliance on external agencies carries significant risks, particularly for women's groups in the Third World whose "resources come from Northern institutions and govern-ments" because they can be used to "blunt the political edge" of feminist organizing (Antrobus 2004, 155).

Members of GABRIELA and other grassroots organizations offered a similar critique when they were approached by the Canadian International Development Agency (CIDA) to participate with women's governmental entities, such as the National Commission on the Role of Filipino Women (NCRFW), on women-in-development projects. In a revealing case study, Nora Angeles examines the tensions underpinning the project, noting that members of grassroots formations were more critical of the government and donor agencies than their mainstream counterparts were (2003, 291). Attributing their stance to their affiliation with the broader nationalist movement, Angeles concludes that those on the "radical left" had become "out of touch with local realities and alienated from official state chan-nels," whereas those on the "moderate left" displayed a greater amount of nuance and complexity when negotiating with local and government agen-cies (2003, 297). Angeles's dismissal of the critiques issued by grassroots aggregations has the potential to leave the underpinning motives behind foreign government agencies such as CIDA unexamined. Considering the asymmetrical relationship between Canada and the Philippines, question-ing the role of the Canadian state and the function of "aid" in a global context are reasonable concerns. Indeed, some Filipino critics warned that the flood of foreign money into women's organizations could possibly lead to the "erosion of feminist militancy, a watering down of leftist explications of women's socio-economic troubles, or the ultimate abandonment of a revolutionary platform" (Aguilar 1997, 313). Compounding these concerns was the weakening state of the Philippine Left, debilitated over the recent years by increasing division among its members.

Some of the tensions among certain women's organizations at the time were rooted in conflicts within the broader nationalist movement.

By 1993, these internal disagreements led to a "split" in the Communist Party, thus triggering a series of changes throughout Philippine Left politics. Documenting this rift in *The Communist Party of the Philippines 1968–1993*, Kathleen Weekley argues the CPP's troubles were ultimately rooted in its adherence to revolutionary Marxist theory and praxis. Illustrative of a postmodernist critique of the "totalizing" framework of Marxism, Weekley explains that the class politics espoused by the CPP excluded a "plethora of cultural and political identities," thereby limiting the effectiveness of its actual practice (2001, 6). The CPP's errors could have been avoided, Weekley asserts, had they abandoned the modernist Marxist paradigm in favor of a postmodern politics of identity capable of recognizing multiple and shifting sites of struggle (2001, 4). In her estimation, the "crisis of Marxism" and the demise of the modern nation-state demonstrate the inadequacy of revolutionary movements reliant on historical materialist analyses of class exploitation.

Women's involvement in the CPP and in the broader national democratic movement is not examined in Weekley's history. She notes, however, that the woman question "is one of the areas of Party discourse which has, through the determined efforts of a few women members and their supporters, noticeably improved over the years" (2001, 11). Though it might be tempting to draw comparisons between Weekley's assessment of the CPP's exclusionary tendencies and those that occurred earlier among Filipino progressives regarding the woman question in Philippine Left politics, there are important and substantive distinctions between the two. For one, by highlighting the sexism endemic in the revolutionary movement and Philippine society at large, Filipino women were not advocating for the abandonment of the class struggle and/or analysis.

Instead, the vigorous debates their critiques provoked illustrated the importance of incorporating feminism within a historical materialist perspective. In contrast, Weekley, among other postmodern intellectuals, substitutes systemic forms of analyses with an eclectic postmodern politics of difference whereby class is emptied of its explanatory potential and redefined as a "cultural" identity interchangeable with gender, race, sexuality, ethnicity, and so on. The rationale behind this theoretical move is to ensure the simultaneous recognition of multiple differences and social struggles. What gets obscured in this theoretical reformulation, however, is an analysis of the productive forces responsible for the creation and maintenance of the differences being discussed. In short, totalizing theories such as Marxism are relegated to the analytical dustbin and replaced by an antifoundational identity politics.

As the early history of the Philippine women's movement reveals, however, dispensing with an analysis of systemic inequality was not an option. That is, despite the well-documented limitations in orthodox Marxist thought, Filipino women worked to expand and reformulate a class analysis that was attendant to the ideological and cultural oppression of women. By redefining feminism in a Third World context and embedding it within the larger national democratic movement, Filipino women created a dynamic, exciting social movement informed by a specific nationalist feminist ideology. As a result of this engagement with the woman question, the women's movement, including those organizations most closely associated with the party, was able to gain a level of autonomy that enabled it to continue to develop its analysis and evolve despite the challenges plaguing the Left. Commenting on the 1995 UN women's conference in Beijing, West and Kwiatkowski observe that GABRIELA's participation "belied charges that it was simply a left-wing or nationalist 'front,' for it demonstrated that its goals remained focused on women" (1997, 159). The evolution of an autonomous women's movement in the Philippines, exemplified by both GABRIELA and the plethora of feminist organizations operating outside the scope of its coalition, challenge contemporary Western feminist narratives that deny the possibility of envisioning and creating nationalist feminist frameworks.

In a departure from some of the existing literature on the subject, Ranjoo Seodu Herr's essay "The Possibility of Nationalist Feminism" revisits some of these earlier debates, arguing that the feminist disavowal of nationalist projects appears too "premature" in light of global socioeconomic realities (2003, 139). Utilizing Anthony Smith's conception of "polycentric" nationalism, which asserts that "one's nation has the right to 'join the family of nations, the international drama of status of equals,'" Herr maintains that nationalism is useful for Third World feminist projects if women "demand that feminist and nationalist goals be pursued simultaneously" (2003, 139, 142). Moreover, Herr explains that once national liberation is achieved, women's interests must continue to be pursued. In the case of the Philippines, the women's movement has achieved relative success in pushing the nationalist movement to recognize women's subjugation as a related concern. In fact, the movement's efforts in the national democratic movement during the late 1970s through the 1980s illustrated that women's liberation was a requirement for national liberation. Though the convergence between feminism and nationalism has often been fraught with tensions and contradictions, the evolution of an autonomous women's movement in the Philippines ensures that the particular condition of women's oppression will continue to be addressed.

Although I agree with many of Herr's points, I wish to point out that the "possibility" of nationalist feminism has been in the process of being realized for the past several decades in the Philippines. This important, yet often neglected history in the canon of transnational feminist thought challenges Herr's observation that she knows "of no actual alliance formed between nationalism and feminism" to combat the deleterious effects of economic globalization (2003, 154). As the following chapters demonstrate, the multisectoral nationalist feminist movement has worked tirelessly to illustrate the critical connections between neoliberal capitalist expansion and Filipino women's exploitation at home and abroad as domestic workers, nurses, nannies, and "entertainers" in this era of global economic restructuring.

Chapter Three

---œœœ---

FROM BALIKBAYANS TO "SUPERMAIDS"

The Gendering of the Philippine Export State

> The better to work here in a house full of faces I don't recognize.
> Shame is less of a burden if spoken in the
> language of soap and stain.
> My whole country cleans houses for food, so that
> the cleaning ends with the mothers, and the daughters will
> have someone clean for them, and never leave
> my country to spend years of conversation with dirt.
> —*Bino A. Realuyo, "Filipineza"*

The inspiration for Realuyo's poignant poem is drawn from a modern Greek dictionary, compiled by George Babiniotis in 1998, that defines "Filipineza" as a "domestic worker from the Philippines or person that performs non-essential auxiliary tasks." In the 1980s there were rumors that the esteemed *Oxford English Dictionary* had a similar entry. Even though this eventually proved to be untrue, the Philippine government expressed outrage that a comparable, pejorative representation of Filipino women was circulating in Greece. Exasperated that "Filipina" had essentially become synonymous with "maid," state officials scrambled to counter the definition by offering various examples of the noteworthy accomplishments Filipino women had achieved over the years. Despite the protests and public indignation, however, the association of Filipino women with domestic help and/or "service"-related occupations persists in the international popular imagination.

Most recently, this was evidenced in an episode of the BBC comedy series *Harry and Paul.* Broadcast to viewers September 2008, the show depicts a Filipino woman dressed in a maid's uniform sexually gyrating around a man (Paul Whitehouse) sitting on a chair in the middle of a yard. From a distance, Harry (Harry Enfield) is observed gesturing and shouting directions at the woman, when a postman arrives to deliver his mail, only to be distracted by the spectacle on the lawn. Harry explains the situation by stating, "Our chums down the road wanted to see if we could mate their Filipino maid with our northener, but he's not having any of it." Irritated by the man's lack of interest, Harry barks, "Come on Clyde! Mount her!" Turning his attention back to the woman, he instructs, "You, you. Present your rear." At this point, the audience watches the woman turn and shake her backside in the northerner's face, while cooing about his "sexiness." After their "experiment" fails, Harry commands the woman to return to her employer's house, as the postman, apparently aroused by her gyrations, hurriedly leaves to escort her down the street. The Philippine Embassy, along with Filipino migrant organizations, immediately protested to the British government for airing the episode, describing it as a "slur against their national character" (Revoir 2008). Similar to the October 2007 debacle involving the ABC series *Desperate Housewives* where Teri Hatcher's character, Susan Mayer, asks to see the medical diplomas of her attending physician to "make sure they're not from some med school in the Philippines," BBC, like ABC, issued a formal apology to the Philippine government.

As these events were unfolding, the World Economic Forum released its 2007 "gender equity" index, wherein the Philippines maintained its sixth place ranking for a second consecutive year. Based on information compiled annually from international agencies, the forum measures a country's progress toward closing the gender gap between men and women in four main categories: political representation, education, wages, and health (MacInnis and Nebehay 2007). While the ranking of the United States dropped eight spots to thirty-one as a result of a weakened economy, the Philippines retained its high position due to "better economic participation ratios" (2007). Two months later, the Association of Southeast Asian Nations commended the Philippines for its "success in closing the gender gap and by promoting human development opportunities" (NCRFW 2008). The NCRFW pledged to use the ranking to "continue the Philippine government's efforts to boost gender equality and women's empowerment in the country" (2008). In a year otherwise marked by political corruption, government scandal, and continuing human rights violations, the forum's annual index was undoubtedly welcome news to the embattled administration of Philippine president Gloria Macapagal-Arroyo. However, the derogatory representations of Filipinas arising from their diasporic jobs as global service workers glaringly reveal the incongruities between the realities of their lives in the world economy and the gender equity report.

Thus, to put the forum's findings in perspective, one could argue that the much-touted increase in economic participation among women directly correlates to their deployment abroad as OFWs. As the Philippine economy continues to buckle under a $54 billion external debt burden (Freedom from Debt Coalition 2007), the prospects of finding full-time employment in the country are increasingly difficult, thus prompting many to leave their families to find work abroad. Currently, 8 million Filipinos (70 percent of whom are women) leave the Philippines to work in low-paying service-oriented occupations as domestic workers, nurses, nannies, and entertainers. Representing the largest source of foreign exchange, the remittances of OFWs—totaling $12–13 billion a year—keep the Philippine economy afloat. The importance of these economic contributions is not lost on Philippine officials, with the past three presidential administrations declaring OFWs to be the "new heroes" of the nation (Aquino), "internationally shared resources" (Ramos), and "overseas Filipino investors" (Arroyo). In 2006, when the Arroyo administration unveiled plans for a training program to upgrade the "skills and knowledge" of Filipino domestic workers, thereby transforming them from "ordinary" maids into "supermaids," the possibility of overseas migration becoming a permanent feature of Philippine economic development strategy appeared likely (Arao 2006, 1).

Among the numerous recruitment and placement agencies whose livelihoods depend upon the availability of a mobile labor pool, Arroyo's supermaid proposition was certainly well received. Utilizing emerging technologies that expedite the matching process for both prospective employers and employees, businesses such as 1maidHK.com have turned to the Internet to advertise their services and "products." For example, interested parties searching for domestic workers can now go to the popular video-sharing site YouTube and type the words "domestic helper" into the search engine to discover an abundance of video advertisements sponsored by 1maidHK.com. These ads feature Filipina women delivering brief descriptions of their personal, educational, and family backgrounds as well as their areas of "expertise" in the household work industry. Describing the company as the "fastest growing internet marketing domestic helper agency" specializing in Filipino domestic helpers, 1maidHK.com strives to make the process easier for potential employers so that they "can find the best domestic helper for their family" (www.1maidHK.com). Based in Hong Kong, the company's Web site offers an "Info Center" that compares the characteristics of Filipino, Indonesian, and Thai domestic helpers. Considered the best option for employers, Filipino women are described as well educated, fluent in English, and "quick learners" with extensive experience working overseas (www.1maidHK.com). According to the operators, these qualities ensure Filipino women will be more "hygienic" than some of the other nationalities offered, thus making them the preferred choice of the agency (www.1maidHK.com). Once more, demeaning representations of Filipino women, premised upon essentialist, racist, and sexist stereotypes, sustain the global trade of their services, ensuring a steady supply of remittance flows back to the already fragile Philippine economy.

These trends in Filipino migration are likely to shift, however, in light of the global financial crisis, specifically the worsening U.S. economy. According to the Philippine Overseas Employment Administration, January 2009 began with the displacement of over 5,000 OFWs in fifteen countries "since the global economic downturn in September 2008" (Africa 2009, 1). For a nation addicted to a steady diet of remittances, the recent economic instability could prove disastrous, exposing the flaws of a neoliberal development approach premised entirely upon the institutionalization of an export-oriented economy. Indeed, the impact of the crisis could explain why, in the 2009 gender equity report, the Philippines dropped three places to number nine. Despite this, it still manages to retain the highest ranking among Asian countries.

With approximately 10 percent of the population currently scattered across 197 countries, the present-day labor export policy of the Philippines can be directly traced to the reckless economic strategies pursued during the Marcos dictatorship (1965–1986). The graft and corruption that characterized this period were primarily responsible for hastening the downward economic spiral the country found itself in after President Diosdado Macapagal arranged for a $300 million "stabilization loan" from the International Monetary Fund in 1962. This, in addition to the devaluation of the peso and the lifting of controls on foreign exchange, marked the beginning of the WB- and IMF-mandated economic "liberalization" program in the Philippines that has had devastating consequences for the majority of the population. According to economist James Boyce, the development plan pursued during this period typified "immizerizing growth" whereby the poor become poorer and "growth itself [became] a cause of impoverishment" (1993, 4). It is estimated that between "1975 and 1985 the incidence of poverty had risen from 46 percent of the population to 52 percent, and in that time 12 million additional people had become 'absolutely poor'" (Pomeroy 1992, 254).

As Ferdinand Marcos was busy depleting the public coffers, the worsening conditions throughout the cities and countryside galvanized the masses as they organized to demand genuine economic, social, and political reform. Student demonstrations in 1970, otherwise known as the First Quarter Storm, were the beginning of more coordinated acts of resistance against the excesses and abuses of the Marcos administration. To quell the growing opposition movement, Marcos declared martial law September 21, 1972. During this time, the United States provided millions of dollars in military aid to shore up his dictatorship as he looted the national treasury and committed widespread human rights abuses against his critics, leading many to characterize this period as the "U.S.-Marcos dictatorship." Five American presidents watched the Marcos regime rob the "Philippine people of between $5 and $10 billion," but "through it all Marcos remained Washington's man in Manila" (Bonner 1988, 6–7). The imposition of martial law also enabled Marcos to embark on a development strategy that involved large-scale borrowing from international lending agencies. Contrary to Marcos's belief that "borrowed money would speed the growth of the Philippine economy" and improve the "well-being of present and future generations of Filipinos," (Boyce 1993,

245), the free-market ideology espoused by Marcos and external creditors led the Philippines into a debilitating state of dependence and indebtedness. In exchange for the loans, the Philippines was forced to comply with structural adjustment programs (SAPs) set forth by the IMF and WB that required major cuts in basic social services in favor of concessions and incentives to foreign investment. The cornerstone of the adjustment program rested on restructuring the Philippine economy toward export-oriented production. A few months after declaring martial law, Marcos established the Bataan Export Processing Zone (EPZ), signaling his adherence to the neoliberal philosophy of export-led industrialization. Although free-trade zones contribute very little to the development and growth of the domestic economy, they were and continue to be vital centers of production for the global economic system.

Agricultural reform was another issue tackled during the martial law era, with a number of presidential decrees issued to encourage the development of agriculturally based exports. Soon, transnational agribusinesses such as Dole and Del Monte began relocating to the Philippines, resulting in the reduction of rice acreage and the displacement of farmers from their land. According to the World Bank, these sacrifices were necessary because the Philippines would soon be transformed into the "food bowl of Asia" (Pomeroy 1992, 253). What these economic advisers failed to mention, however, is that these agricultural exports, often produced by the intensive exploitation of Philippine labor, were never intended for "consumption by the Filipino people, the vast majority of whom cannot afford to sup from the 'food bowl'" (Pomeroy 1992, 253). Consequently, these so-called reforms led to an increase in poverty and malnutrition, thus prompting a wave of internal migration as rural Filipinos began moving to urban centers in search of work.

As is often the case in a faltering economy, women and children bear the brunt of such crises. Seen merely as an auxiliary or secondary workforce, they have typically been the first to be laid off during economic hardship and the last to be reabsorbed, thereby creating a reserve army of labor. Throughout the Marcos era, many Filipino women had to seek work either within the informal sector of the economy or abroad in search of waged employment. To illustrate the human costs of large-scale borrowing, Sylvia Chant and Cathy McIlwaine estimate that contributions to the gross national product from the informal sector increased from

26 percent in 1960 to 48 percent in 1988, with over half the population relegated to laboring in this sector (1995, 70). Another option for some of the most impoverished families was to send young, single, female relatives to find jobs in the various factories and EPZs throughout the cities. Transnational corporations (TNCs) have a lengthy history of utilizing racial, ethnic, and gender stereotypes to recruit young women, often perceived as a "cheap" and "docile" workforce, to work in their firms. By categorizing young women's labor as "unskilled," TNCs are able to effectively confine women to labor-intensive, low-paying jobs with little room for advancement.

In many ways, the situation of Filipino women during the 1970s and 1980s mirrored that of other Third World women who were being subjected to the onerous conditions of IMF/WB-imposed SAPs. Indeed, the gendered consequences of neoliberal capitalist development programs were felt most acutely among women living in the global South, thus serving to "radicalize large sections of women's movements worldwide" (Antrobus 2004, 68). As the previous chapter demonstrated, Filipino women were actively organizing around a range of issues throughout this time. Informing their analysis of women's oppression was an understanding of how macroeconomic policies imposed by the West, particularly the United States, affected women's lives in all spheres of a given society. Peggy Antrobus suggests that the consequences of such initiatives were more than "merely economic" because their abandonment of social development meant that the needs of the labor force necessary to promote fiscal growth could not be met, thus undermining the "very basis for economic production and productivity" (2004, 69). In the case of the Philippines, the social and cultural changes wrought by IMF/WB intervention during the Marcos dictatorship are still manifest today, evidenced by the staggering number of citizens applying for overseas work.

Initially, the LEP was created as a temporary measure to stave off unemployment and stimulate the economy. Often referred to as the "warm body export," Marcos institutionalized labor exportation in 1974, with the majority of Filipino migrants made up of men working in construction and other related jobs throughout the Middle East. By the 1980s, however, Filipino migration had become feminized, as more women left the country to work primarily as domestic helpers in the affluent countries of the global North. In 1982, recognizing the importance of remittances to servicing the ballooning external debt, the Marcos regime issued Executive Order (EO) 857 mandating that overseas workers remit 50–70 percent of their salaries back to the Philippines through the Central Bank. If workers failed to comply, the government would not renew their passports, effectively preventing them from working overseas. Outraged by the punitive nature of the measure, Filipina domestic workers in Hong Kong banded together with eleven other Filipino migrant organizations in 1984 to form United Filipino Workers Against Forced Remittance (UNFARE—United Filipino Workers in Hong Kong). As a result of their collective efforts, Marcos repealed the legislation in 1985, granting UNFARE an important victory. The success of their mass action campaign against EO 857 led UNFARE members to formally launch the United Filipinos in Hong Kong alliance, a coalition of various groups that continues to advocate on behalf of migrant workers today.

Throughout the decade, the number of Filipino migrant nongovernmental organizations began to swell as reports of growing abuses against Filipina workers became more widespread. A survey conducted during this period revealed that the majority of domestic helpers suffered "extreme degradation, humiliation, sexual harassment [while many were] faced with hazardous working conditions, including contract substitution, wage discrimination, ill treatment by employers and other degrading factors" (Vickers 1994, 90). Established in Hong Kong in 1981, the Mission for Filipino Migrant Workers is considered to be the first organization founded in the region to address the needs of overseas Filipinas "in distress" (Mission for Migrant Workers). Shortly thereafter, several more organizations were created, including the Asian Pacific Mission for Filipino Migrants (1984) and the Bethune House Migrant Women's Refuge (1986), to offer temporary housing, counseling, and legal services to Filipina migrants seeking refuge from abusive employers. The proliferation of so many groups geared toward the specific task of addressing the exploitation of Filipinas reflects the dire situation many women found themselves in while working in their "host" countries.

After Marcos was ousted by the People Power movement in 1986, newly elected president Corazon Aquino was left to deal with the growing outcry over the maltreatment of Filipina overseas workers. In an effort to shield them from further abuse, she issued a temporary ban on Filipina entertainers traveling to Japan and a similar decree in 1988 halting the deployment of Filipina domestic helpers (de Guzman 2003, 3). For migrant advocates, however, such measures did more harm to Filipino women because limited employment opportunities in the country would force many to migrate illegally, thus placing them in even more precarious situations (2003, 3). Despite lifting the ban under pressure from migrant worker NGOs, the government did very little to address the economic crisis largely responsible for generating the massive outflow of labor power from the country. Having inherited a $28 billion external debt burden from the Marcos dictatorship, the Aquino administration recognized overseas worker remittances as one of the most reliable sources of foreign exchange necessary to keeping the Philippine economy from slipping further into bankruptcy. Even though she recognized the sacrifices of migrants by declaring December "The Month of Overseas Filipinos" and labeling OFWs the new "heroes" of the nation, the promotion of labor export as a key to Philippine economic development was continued during the Aquino years.

The steady increase in migration, however, continued to place many Filipinos at risk as the state proved incapable of protecting its citizens from the numerous acts of cruelty and humiliation they experienced abroad. This incompetency was exposed in 1995 when the Singapore government executed Flor Contemplacion, a Filipina domestic worker accused of murdering another Filipina domestic helper and her young ward. In spite of mounting evidence pointing to the innocence of Contemplacion, the Philippine government's failure to intervene to stop her execution prompted national and international protests. At the forefront of the demonstrations were members of Migrante International, a global alliance of migrant organizations formally launched in Manila in 1996. Working closely with some of the migrant worker NGOs, Migrante expanded its network to include Europe, the United States, and Canada (Migrante International). Situating Filipino migration within the uneven development of global capitalism and U.S. imperialism, Migrante lobbied the Philippine government to institute systemic reforms to ensure other overseas workers would not meet the same fate as Contemplacion. As a response to the international outcry, President Fidel Ramos passed Republic Act (RA) 8042, the Migrant Workers and Overseas Filipinos Act of 1995, signaling the state's commitment to providing better services to its overseas population.

In her analysis of this particular period, Robyn Rodriguez examines the internal negotiations, what she describes as the "domestic debates" (2008, 2), that ensued between state and civil society actors in the aftermath of Contemplacion's death. According to her, the discourse of both state officials and feminist-oriented migrant NGOs dovetailed in rendering migrant women workers helpless "victims" in need of state "protection." In their effort to get migrant reform laws enacted, she argues, both entities reproduced traditional patriarchal notions of "femininity." For example, interviews and surveys conducted by state representatives suggest that Filipino women's decision to leave their families and homes behind to care for the needs of others, thereby transgressing conventional expectations of Filipino womanhood, created a deep sense of shame and nationalist anxiety among many Filipinos (Rodriguez 2008). Similarly, Rodriguez noted that the language employed by NGO advocates often cast migrant women as "young" and "innocent," furthering the impression that their decision to work abroad was borne out of naïveté, thus making them more susceptible to abuse. Taken together, Rodriguez concludes that these representations of Filipina overseas workers rest on "specific gendered logics" that "require intervention by the paternal state to prevent them from harming their families and the nation" (2008, 8). Legislation such as RA 8042, therefore, became emblematic of such protection because it appeared more concerned with the "regulation of women migrants themselves" and less interested in "the regulation of women's migration" (2008, 9). In the end, she determines that both the state and migrant NGOs bear equal responsibility for disciplining migrant women's bodies in the service of buttressing patriarchal relations.

The aptly titled essay "Beyond Heroes and Victims" echoes Rodriguez's concern with governmental and nongovernmental representations of migrant Filipino women. Katherine Gibson, Lisa Law, and Deirdre McKay challenge the Philippine government's "nationalist" construction of migrant workers as "heroes" and the NGO "leftist internationalist discourse which represents Filipina contract migrants as 'victims' in a global labour market" (2001, 366). For the authors, the NGO deployment of a "capitalocentric" narrative that connects the present-day exploitation of migrant Filipinas to "prior colonial and neo-colonial relations" serves only to produce a "depressing and potentially disempowering scenario [such that] nothing short of systemic revolution can be envisioned as a way forward" (2001, 381, 371). In other words, what the critics find most objectionable is the anti-imperialist class analysis informing the political praxis of progressive Filipino organizations. Influenced by the post-Marxist work of J. K. Gibson-Graham, the authors argue that the hegemonic capitalist script characterizing the worldview of grassroots NGOs effectively forecloses the possibility of other economic identities and class positions from emerging.

As a corrective to the "static" tendencies posited by both governmental and nongovernmental actors, the writers suggest a theoretical intervention premised upon a fluid, antiessentialist "politics of class becoming" (Gibson, Law, and McKay 2001, 366). In this latest manifestation, the category of class appears as a linguistic construction existing outside the disciplining apparatus of a "totalizing" capitalist system. Gibson, Law, and McKay explain that this redefined "language of class sees a variety of class processes (including slave, feudal, independent, communal, as well as capitalist) coexisting in a diverse economy" (2001, 375). Released from the social relations of production, class power reemerges in "multiple" and "multidirectional" ways, moving representations of Filipina domestic workers beyond the allegedly oppressive binary of "hero" and "victim" to reveal their new identity as "economic activists" in control of their own destiny (2001, 365, 377). Some examples of their economic activism include demanding extra pay from their employers for household duties outside their work contract (such as washing the car) and using savings from their remittances to return to the Philippines to engage in entrepreneurial activities such as opening a *sari-sari* store and/or becoming a landowner with tenants (2001, 377). These locally based, community investment ventures are supported by NGO programs that view the migrant subjects as "full of potentiality rather than lack," thus enabling their diverse economic identities to flourish (2001, 380). Though the authors conclude their essay by acknowledging there is no right or wrong way to approach the subject of Filipino women's migration, they clearly position themselves in opposition to the "left internationalist" perspective offered by certain Filipino migrant NGOs.

I highlight these essays because their critiques of the philosophical and representational practices of certain grassroots groups represent some of the current trends in contemporary feminist theory. Given the country's reputation as one of the largest exporting states of women's labor power, it is not surprising that the Philippines has become the subject of a number of empirical studies on the subject. Following the 1997 publication of Nicole Constable's *Maid to Order in Hong Kong*, a flurry of scholarship focusing on the global dimension of Filipino women's lives appeared: Rhacel Parrenas's *Servants of Globalization* (2001) and *Children of Global Migration* (2005), Neferti Tadiar's *Fantasy-Production* (2004), Catherine Choy's *Empire of Care* (2003), and Emily Ignacio's *Building Diaspora* (2005), to name a few representative examples. Although each of these texts approaches the subject of Filipino women's migration from a specific methodological perspective, what binds the majority of this intellectual work together is their underlying theoretical orientation.

Reflecting the cultural turn in feminist scholarship, Foucauldian-inspired discursive analyses emphasizing overseas Filipino women's "agency" and "resistance" have become the prevailing conceptual lens from which to understand their subordinate position in the global economy. For example, coping mechanisms such as "frowning or crying" are recast by theoreticians as performative acts of resistance done to elicit "emotions among employers (such as discomfort and guilt) which then makes employers more cooperative" (Parrenas 2001, 252). The "diaries, letters and phone calls" sent by domestic workers to their families serve as examples of the "subjective activity of women" (Tadiar 2004, 131, 136). According to Tadiar, these creative pursuits illustrate that "Filipina domestic helpers are not merely objects of other people's practices, objects of better or worse 'treatment,' conservation and regulation; they are active producers and creative mediators of the world in which they move" (2004, 132). Citing the last letter of a domestic worker who died at the hands of her employer, Tadiar explains that her "power" was "enacted through writing to reach beyond the confinements of her bodily labour-time" (2004, 137). For other scholars, such as Choy, the very act of migration exemplifies an "individual and collective desire for a unique form of social, cultural, and economic success obtainable only outside the national borders of the Philippines" (2003, 7). Together, these accounts portray Filipino women as desiring, laboring, and empowered (even in death) subjects in the era of globalization. Often considered cutting edge for their attention to women's subjectivity, these writings mirror the reigning theoretical template in contemporary Filipina American feminist thought.

This focus on the localized activities of individual migrants can be attributed to the transnational framework that underpins the majority of feminist writing in this area. In large part, the adoption of a transnational perspective by critical theorists stems from a disillusionment with the supposedly homogenizing and essentializing characteristics of structuralist analyses. By allegedly reducing all social phenomena to the workings of global capitalism and the social relations of production, transnational scholars argue that the diversity of individual experience is effectively erased. For example, Aihwa Ong laments that studies of globalization have been dominated by totalizing theories of "economic rationality bereft of human agency" (1999, 4). In an early comparative analysis of Filipino and Caribbean migration patterns, the authors of *Nations Unbound* take aim at world system theorists for their inability to recognize that in addition to being workers, migrants "are at the same time political and social actors" (Basch, Schiller, and Blanc 1993, 12). For critics, successfully showcasing the agentive capacities of migrants requires a transnational framework capable of capturing their mobility as they live their lives "stretched across national borders" (1993, 3–8). Accordingly, the concept of "immigrant" has been replaced by "transmigrant" to illustrate the multiple ways individuals sustain contact in both their host and home countries. Thus, for the past several decades, attention to the indeterminate and interstitial spaces occupied by modern-day migrant populations has formed the center of the transnational theoretical enterprise.

The current moment of social, economic, and political crisis in the Philippines provides an important opportunity to assess the efficacy of such knowledge production. My critique of these texts is not meant to minimize the important contributions each has provided to the growth and expansion of Filipina American feminism. Rather, it is intended to draw attention to the numerous ways U.S. imperialism, masked as "globalization," continues to distort and shape the lives of Filipinos at home and abroad. The postmodern-inspired emphasis on agency, resistance, and representation serves to obscure the fundamentally exploitative neocolonial relationship between the United States and the Philippines—the very reason the latter finds itself as one of the chief exporters of women's (cheap) labor power in the world.

Although it is difficult, if not impossible, to write about the Philippines and ignore its lengthy history of Spanish and U.S. colonial subjugation, what matters is the manner in which these issues (imperialism, capitalism, globalization) are theorized in academic accounts. If, as I suggest, Filipina American feminism is reflective of the cultural, or post-modern, turn in Western feminist theory, then it follows that analyses of global capitalism remain confined to the realm of discourse, removed from the social relations of production. As Teresa Ebert explains in her groundbreaking work *Ludic Feminism and After,* "What is at stake in this displacement of the economic by discourse is the elision of issues of exploitation and the substitution of a discursive identity politics for the struggle for full social and economic emancipation" (1996, 42). We see this tendency in Tadiar's work when she discusses the usefulness of Marxism for understanding work and labor but finds the "obstinate refusal of more orthodox Marxisms to factor in categories of gender, race, and sexuality" limiting (2004, 8). As a result, she turns to the psychoanalytic theory of Slavoj Zizek because he "merges the two theoretical discourses of Marxism and psychoanalysis to arrive at an understanding of ideology as an 'unconscious fantasy structuring our social reality itself'" (2004, 9). In this analytic move Zizek, and by default Tadiar, erases "ideology's relation to a materialist base—the forces and economic relations of production—only to substitute in its place a grounding of all ideology, in fact all reality, on the idealist base of enjoyment" (Ebert 1996, 61). Thus, any systemic attempt to understand the Philippines and its dependent peripheral status is obscured by the persistent tendency to negate the material (economic) in favor of the cultural (ideological) (1996, 60–61).

This theoretical obfuscation of class relations is evident in recent accounts of Filipino identity and migration. Choy explains that the "desire of Filipino nurses to migrate abroad cannot be reduced to an economic logic" (2003, 7) as so many other studies of migration have suggested. What differentiates Parrenas's approach to migration from others is her emphasis on the "level of the subject," which enables her to better understand the "limits and possibilities, of agency" (2001, 250–251). As fragmented subjects attempting to reconcile their contradictory position in their "host" country, Filipina migrants unintentionally end up maintaining "inequalities, particularly the system of global restructuring in which their constitution as subjects is situated" (2001, 253). In an interesting theoretical sleight of hand by Parrenas, we discover that the recuperation of power by individual domestic workers makes them unwittingly complicit in their own (as well as others') exploitation by the forces of global capitalism. This diffusion of power, à la Foucault, makes it impossible to ascertain the material realities informing Filipino women's migration or their actions once consigned to living in their host country. As I have written elsewhere (Lacsamana 1998), Constable's study of Filipina domestic workers in Hong Kong is an exemplary model of this particular analytical position. In her conclusion, she maintains that regarding "these women simply as oppressed by those 'with power' is to ignore the subtler and more complex forms of power, discipline, and resistance in their everyday lives" (1997, 202). Though many of these analyses discuss the political economy as a contributing factor to women's migration, the centrality of class is often eclipsed by analytical formulations that recast the phenomenon as a "global care chain" involving the extraction and transfer of "emotional labor" from the Third to the First World (Parrenas 2001; Hochschild 2002). Without denying the important position "care" occupies in enhancing our understanding of women's reproductive work, the preoccupation with "emotion" and "love" has the unintended consequence of minimizing the exploitative and unequal conditions characterizing domestic labor.

A more recent addition to the Filipino migration literature is Ignacio's *Building Diaspora,* an interesting examination of cyber "community-building" among diasporic Filipinos. By analyzing a Filipino Internet newsgroup (soc.culture.filipino), Ignacio explores the representations and various manifestations of Filipino identity. The uniqueness of her study, however, is undermined by the absence of a sociohistorical framework from which to understand the dispersal of Filipinos around the world. Though she touches upon U.S. colonialism in different sections of the text, it is primarily referenced in relation to the "hybrid" formation of Filipino identity. In a review, Filipino American scholar Michael Viola notes that the text "sidesteps significant questions such as: why are more than ten million Filipinos (the majority women) involved in a forced diaspora searching for a 'homeland' away from their concrete conditions in the Philippines? What are the historical origins that have created these conditions?" (2007, 162). Echoing my own concerns with the current body of scholarship on Filipino migration, Viola draws attention to the critical gaps in contemporary transnational theorizing.

Answering such questions would require a return to a systemic analysis that can account for the Philippines' peripheral status vis-à-vis the metropole. I realize advocating for a historical materialist framework runs the risk of being dismissed outright as retrograde in certain feminist circles; however, it remains the most powerful explanatory tool for understanding and transforming the iniquitous power relations between the West and "the rest." Without such an analysis, some could be misled into believing that the majority of Filipino women working as OFWs are freely choosing to migrate thousands of miles away from their homeland and families to labor and live abroad. This is not to suggest that *all* examples of migration are involuntary but merely to point out that the international division of labor wrought by capitalist processes underpins the economic crisis currently plaguing the Philippines, prompting today's "warm body" export.

Describing Filipino migration in terms of an international transference of feminized labor power from the Third World to the First World, Grace Chang's *Disposable Domestics* provides an alternative perspective for understanding the macroeconomic processes informing contemporary migratory flows. Chang makes clear that migration "is not a matter of an individual woman's free choice, but a response to poverty created by First World imperialism and perpetuated by SAPs" (2000, 142). The neoliberal economic dismantling of social welfare supports in countries of both the global North and South have produced a "global exchange" whereby Third World women fill the void in their capacity as an "ideal source of cheap, highly exploitable labor" (2000, 130). Far from being rendered powerless by this exploitation, however, Filipino women have generated an inspiring, collective, grassroots movement among Filipino migrant workers. Similar to the groups mentioned earlier, Chang documents the impressive amount of organizing conducted by migrant rights advocates belonging to GABRIELA and GABRIELA USA, Kalayaan (England), the Commission for Filipino Migrant Workers (the Netherlands), Intercede (Canada), and the Campaign for Migrant Domestic Worker Rights (United States), to name a few. By offering educational workshops on migrant rights, monitoring reports of abuse, and providing legal aid, among other services, these organizations are waging resistance campaigns on behalf of overseas Filipino workers from the ground up.

During a research trip to the Philippines in January 2007, I had the opportunity to visit the headquarters of Migrante International. While there, I met two young women who had been working as domestic workers in Hong Kong. Both had fled their abusive employers and were seeking refuge at Migrante until their cases were filed with the proper authorities. I also learned of numerous campaigns to free Filipino women who were being illegally detained in Lebanon and others who were facing execution on trumped-up charges. In an interview with Migrante's chairperson, Connie Bragas Regaldo, she explained that the maldevelopment of the Philippine economy, compounded by the ongoing war in Mindanao, has displaced many Filipinos from their land and livelihood, forcing them to migrate from the provinces to the cities and then overseas in search of employment. Speaking as a former domestic helper who worked in Hong Kong, Regaldo explained that if "there is a chance to stay in the Philippines, to have a decent job ... I don't want to leave my country, to leave my family" (2007). For her, migration is "forced" upon Filipinos as a result of high unemployment, foreign development projects, and a government-instituted labor-only contracting policy that has transformed the nation into a workforce of low-wage, part-time, flexible laborers for transnational companies. As a result of these conditions, it is estimated that approximately 3,400 Filipinos leave the country each day, with 6 to 8 returning in coffins. According to Regaldo, if one were to include the number of undocumented workers departing the country on "tourist" visas, the overall figures for OFWs would increase dramatically.

I flashed upon her comments a few months later while conducting research on Filipino migrants in Europe. Having traveled to Amsterdam to meet with members of Migrante-Europe, I had the occasion to speak with some undocumented Filipino workers. Specifically, I recall a conversation I had with two women, both of whom had traveled to the Netherlands over ten years before on tourist visas and never returned home. Their stories painted a vivid picture of lives lived underground, identities rendered invisible by the conditions of their itinerant labor status. Through informal networks, each had initially taken jobs as caregivers or nannies, only to discover they were expected to work full time as live-in domestic workers. Though they never described their employers as "abusive," they frequently complained of the various "extra" tasks and duties they were expected to do as part of their jobs. As they spoke, I was reminded of Bridget Anderson's analysis of the vexed relationship between employer and domestic helper. Because the domestic worker reproduces "people and social relations," Anderson argues that "it is not just her labour power that is being harnessed to the cause of her employer's physical and social reproduction, but it is the very fact that *she,* the domestic worker, and not her employers, is doing this work, much of which seems invented for her especially to do. The employer is buying the power to command, not the property in person, but the whole person" (2000, 113).

In this rich and textured examination of the racialized and gendered dimensions of domestic work, Anderson's suggestion that it is a woman's personhood, rather than simply her labor power, that is being purchased by employers highlights the particularly exploitative and exhausting nature of this type of employment. Moreover, her examination challenges the "emotional labor" paradigm by warning scholars of the inherent danger involved with conflating "care as labour and care as emotion" (2000, 116). For Anderson, the inability to distinguish between the two categories can "lead to an argument that care is not exploitative because women want to do it … and because they are doing it of their own free will" (2000, 116). In the specific case of domestic work, the lens of care obscures the physical toll of the labor involved, negating the iniquitous relationship between employers and employed (2000, 116–121).

Unable to continue working as "live-in" domestic helpers because of the constant demands and conditions of their employment, both of the women I spoke with were juggling several part-time jobs in the service industry to make ends meet. Despite the pain of being separated from their families, and the insecurity of their everyday existence as undocumented workers, neither had plans to return to the Philippines. Reflecting a common trend among women migrants, the decision not to return to their home countries has led some scholars to conclude that their reluctance is not solely due to "poverty" but rather is related to a fear of losing the "freedom" and "independence" they have gained through the migratory process (Parrenas 2001; Ehrenreich and Hochschild 2002; Hondagneu-Sotelo 1994). For the women I spoke with, however, low wages and limited job opportunities in the Philippines were the overwhelming reasons that they remained in the Netherlands. Their situation might be altered, however, as a result of recent immigration legislation sponsored by the European Union that specifically targets undocumented workers. Referred to as the Employer Sanction Directive, the law will penalize employers for hiring "illegal" workers and encourage "overstaying aliens" to voluntarily leave or face legal detention (del Callar 2009). For the estimated 113,000 "illegal Pinoys" in Europe, this new law means a return to a "bleak future" because the Philippines is unable to offer any source of stable employment (2009).

At present, ensuring the welfare of OFWs in the wake of the current global economic collapse has now become a top priority for migrant rights advocates. In addition to sponsoring legislation requesting the establishment of a "contingency fund" for recently laid-off migrants, members of GWP have urged the government to place a moratorium on the onerous processing fees OFWs have to pay prior to leaving the country (GWP 2009). Similarly, the Migrante Sectoral Party, now headed by Regaldo, seeks to hold the Philippine government responsible for the safety and welfare of OFWs by sponsoring a variety of initiatives aimed at shifting the financial burden of OFW services back to the state instead of the worker (Adams 2009, 2). Pursuing a multipronged approach, activists understand that their legislative efforts provide only "temporary relief" to migrant workers, recognizing that systemic reform is necessary to tackling the underlying causes responsible for Filipino overseas migration. Nevertheless, as Regaldo states, the existence of their political organization ensures that the "once disenfranchised migrant workers have their own political voice" (Adams 2009, 2).

As the economy continues to deteriorate with growing unemployment and joblessness throughout the country, the international capitalist crisis exposes the current dissonance between contemporary trends in knowledge production and the everyday material realities confronting those living in the global South. Arguably, the transformative and liberatory potential of feminist criticism has been deradicalized by the ascendency of "post" theories in the Western academy over the past twenty years. In this case, the historical inequality and violence characterizing U.S.-Philippine relations are flattened or leveled to showcase the mobility of the subalterns as they struggle to make ends meet. Theorists, effectively delinking migrant workers from the sociopolitical forces responsible for their condition, neatly repackage their nomadic existences into transgressive acts of desire, power, and pleasure. Within this reigning theoretical purview, attention to structural forms of oppression and collective acts of resistance has been replaced by a focus on discursive abstractions emphasizing the quotidian, micropolitics of everyday life, thereby severing intellectual production from those collectively organizing for social justice outside the academy. In contrast, by center-staging the pernicious effects of neoliberal capitalist development in the Philippines and the resulting failure of the country to provide adequate jobs for its citizens, the oft-criticized "capitalocentric" lens of grassroots migrant groups seems as timely as ever. More importantly, however, the numerous examples of their mass organizing challenges those analyses that contend macroeconomic perspectives strip individuals of their agency, rendering them helpless, passive bystanders in the face of global economic forces. As the next chapters illustrate, the anti-imperialist, nationalist feminist framework informing the political praxis of Filipino women's grassroots groups is an effective strategy for combating the related ills of prostitution and U.S. military violence in the Philippine context.

Chapter Four

∞

PROSTITUTED WOMEN

Revisiting the Sex Work Debates in Feminist Theory

> Tourism, a big dollar earner for the country, has had for its
> main attraction and commodity the Filipino woman.
> —*Aida F. Santos, Do Women Really
> Hold Up Half the Sky?*

In addition to the labor export program, another important cornerstone
of Philippine "development" during the Marcos period was the promotion of tourism as a means to generate foreign exchange. For Ferdinand
Marcos, both the economic and political benefits of tourism were crucial
to ensuring his stronghold over the country throughout his dictatorship.
As evidence of this, the Ministry of Tourism was established in 1973,
one year after the declaration of martial law, and was headed by a close
ally, Jose Aspiras. With the help of loans obtained from the World Bank,
the Ministry of Tourism oversaw the construction of "fourteen first-class
hotels and a luxurious conference center in Manila at a cost of over $450
million" (Schirmer and Shalom 1987, 182). Though these building projects were excessive and at a great cost to the Philippine people, the regime
felt that "luxurious accommodations and political stability generated good

71

will among foreign business people and international bankers whose support [they] needed" (1987, 182). As it turns out, however, it was not the extravagant accommodations that became the central feature of Philippine tourism. Instead, the state used the "reputed beauty and generosity of Filipino women as 'natural resources' to compete in the international tourist market" (Enloe 1990, 38; Lacsamana 2004).

The commodification of Filipino women's sexuality turned out to be a profitable marketing strategy, with various indicators revealing a direct correlation between the growth in prostitution throughout Manila and other popular tourist areas in the country and the rise in international tourism. Elizabeth Eviota explains that by the late 1970s, Philippine tourism was bringing in "$300,000,000, which [was] $262,000,000 more than in 1972" (1992, 137). By the mid-1980s, the majority of tourists in the Philippines were Japanese, Australian, and American men who had traveled to the country as part of a "sex tour." Included in a typical sex tour package were brochures of women that men could select from, transportation to the various "girlie bars" throughout Manila, and accommodations at some of the most posh hotels either owned or financed by government officials. The collusion among top-ranking government officials, tour operators, and local law enforcement agencies enabled prostitution to flourish. Although the state repeatedly denied any connection between the increase in prostitution and the development of tourism as an "industry," evidence to the contrary was overwhelming. Linda Richter explains that the administration's lack of intervention in the sex trade included a "*quid pro quo*: unflinching support of the administration from the tourist industry" (1982, 143). For example, during the 1978 parliamentary election "Minister Aspiras called all major hotel and tour operators together ... and pressured them to instruct their employees to vote for the administration, because the opposition would destroy the tourist industry" (1982, 143). Characteristic of the Marcos years, this level of corruption and bribery ensured his regime would remain in power and prostitution would remain untouched (Lacsamana 2004).

Since the 1980s, however, because of campaigns waged both inside and outside the Philippines, the number of sex tours has declined significantly. As a result, the "hospitality" industry has returned in different forms: Women now migrate overseas as "brides," "artists," and "entertainers." In the case of the latter, the Philippine Overseas Employment Agency offers training in the performing arts for those wishing to become "overseas performance artists." Sheila Jeffreys reports that in 2004 "eighty thousand Filipinas entered Japan on six month entertainment visas" enabling them to remit $250 million back to the Philippines (2009, 5). In an already strapped economy buckling under the weight of an international recession, it is not difficult to understand why the Philippine government continues to actively promote overseas migration in all its forms. Nor is it any wonder that prostitution and trafficking have remained pressing issues for the bulk of Filipino feminist organizations.

As a credit to their sustained efforts over the past several decades, the Philippines joined a growing number of countries that recently instituted legislation aimed at curbing and/or eradicating human trafficking with the passage of the Anti-Trafficking in Persons Act of 2003 (RA 9208). Dovetailing with the UN International Convention Against Transnational Organized Crime (2000), specifically the accompanying UN Protocol to Prevent, Suppress, and Punish Trafficking in Persons, Especially Women and Children (2003), the Philippine government's adoption of RA 9208 provides us with an important opportunity to revisit the ongoing international feminist debates concerning trafficking, prostitution, sex work, and women's agency. As I've written elsewhere (Lacsamana 2004), feminist thought has undergone a significant shift over the past twenty or so years around the subject of prostitution, with the dominant paradigm articulating a "sex work" position that emphasizes both the legitimacy of prostitution as work and the freedom and agency of women involved in the industry. This position contrasts with those who seek to eradicate prostitution on the grounds that it is an inherently exploitative and violent practice rooted in unequal patriarchal and material relations. Thus, how one perceives the recent spate of international and national laws aimed at ending the "traffic in women" largely depends on one's political and theoretical perspective.

I situate these debates within the Philippine context, noting that the majority of contemporary scholarship produced by feminist practitioners is clearly, once more, at odds with the bulk of Filipino feminist activism and organizing around trafficking and prostitution. Indeed, as I detail in the remainder of this chapter, it is the specific ideological and political practice underpinning the efforts of certain Filipino women's NGOs that has garnered a significant amount of criticism from those theoreticians advocating a sex work analysis. The source of this schism, I argue, stems directly from the cultural turn in feminist thought. Similar to the work produced on Filipino women's migration, this mode of thinking has deliberately eschewed accounts that seek to radically transform the structural mechanisms (neoliberal capitalism, [neo]colonialism, imperialism, militarism, etc.) largely responsible for the worldwide growth in commercialized sexual activities in favor of analyses focused on the complexity of individual women's subjectivity and resistance. In short, this has led to a depoliticized brand of feminist thinking, content with interpreting and translating everyday acts of survival into symbols of women's liberation and empowerment.

Though it is difficult to trace an exact "moment" when feminists became divided over the subject, one could argue that the 1982 Scholar and Feminist IX Conference "Towards a Politics of Sexuality" held at Barnard College in New York helped to usher in the "sex wars" and the "pro-sex/pro-sex work" framework that has now become commonplace in feminist scholarship. For example, the publication of *Good Girls/Bad Girls* (Bell) in 1987 was followed by several other works, including *Sex Work* (Delacoste and Alexander 1987), *A Vindication of the Rights of Whores* (Pheterson 1989), *Whores and Other Feminists* (Nagle 1997), and *Global Sex Workers* (Kempadoo and Doezema 1998). Although this list is a mere sampling of the range of writing on the subject, it is indicative of how pervasive this particular analytical lens became during the late twentieth century.

Global Sex Workers, edited by Kamala Kempadoo and Jo Doezema, is among the first anthologies to apply a sex work analysis to conditions facing women and children in the Third World. Their use of the phrase "sex worker" is a deliberate theoretical strategy that locates prostitution "not as an identity—a social or psychological characteristic of women, often indicated by 'whore'—but as an income-generating activity or form of labor for women and men. The definition stresses the social location of those engaged in sex industries as 'working people'" (1998, 3). Arguing against those who view the sale of sex as harmful and exploitative, Kempadoo explains that such a perspective confuses "the sale of one's sexual energy ... with a particular morality about sexual relations," thereby imposing "essentialist cultural interpretations upon the subject" (1998, 5). This perspective is in stark contrast to Filipino women's organizations like GABRIELA, Development Action for Women Network, and the

CATW-AP, whose members employ the term "prostituted" women to highlight iniquitous power relationships and external material conditions responsible for many women's entrance into the commercialized sex industry. By deploying the concept of "emotional labor," which supposedly enables sex workers to "distinguish intimacy and love from the sex act itself, much in the same way an actor or therapist is able to separate their work from private life, preserving a sense of integrity and distance from emotionally demanding work" (Kempadoo and Doezema 1998, 5), the sex work position effectively flattens differences between "workers" based on a range of social categories, including race, class, and nation, in order to highlight how those engaged in the industry enact personal forms of agency.

Lisa Law's essay "Dancing on the Bar" is an illustrative example of how this particular perspective works when applied to Filipino women in the sex industry. Given the complex and interrelated history of U.S. imperialism and militarism throughout the country (a subject I discuss in greater detail in the following chapter), Law acknowledges the difficulty of analyzing the commodification of Filipino women's sexuality "without at least contemplating the structural inequalities and patterns of globalization which have enabled the development of sex industries catering to foreign men" (1997, 107). Though she credits the "important interpretive frames provided by feminist, nationalist and anti-colonial accounts of sex tourism" for "highlighting the economic, political and social bases of inequality," she argues that such advocacy work "reinforces the hegemonically constructed identities of the 'oppressor' and the 'victim' through naturalizing them as fixed identities and subject positions" (1997, 107). Indeed, as is often the case with this brand of thinking, those activists working to transform the structural conditions responsible for the proliferation of the sex trade end up being accused of creating stereotypical accounts that rely on a "rich-Western-male/poor-Filipina-female dichotomy" (1997, 107). For Law, the "deterministic" approach toward prostitution provided by "middle-class activists" obscures the "potential to locate where more subtle sites of resistance are enunciated" (1997, 108–109). Accordingly, then, Western men who travel to the Philippines to visit go-go bars should not be seen as merely oppressors seeking to exploit Filipino women's sexuality, nor should Filipino women be characterized as powerless victims devoid of agency. Further, to describe such men as "customers" and women as "prostitutes" reinforces dualistic thinking that obfuscates the complex, ambivalent play of power.

Utilizing Homi Bhaba's (1994) concept of "third space" where identities are in flux rather than fixed and dichotomies are replaced by fluidities, Law applies this idea to the physical place of the Philippine go-go bar. Rather than a site where men (primarily Western) go to see Filipino women dance, it is reinterpreted as "an ambivalent space of negotiation, and a site of struggle for meaning and representation" (1997, 111). In the go-go bar/third space, the act of dancing on the bar enables Filipino women to "resist the power of the voyeuristic gaze through disruption rather than covert opposition" (1997, 111). Though it is never made clear how, exactly, power relations between Western men and Filipino women are disrupted, Law's argument is in keeping with the postmodern ethos of shunning totalizing or explanatory frameworks, leaving it to readers to fashion their own interpretations. Her discussion of sex tourism in the Philippines follows a familiar template in contemporary feminist thought.

In a critique of Kempadoo's "Slavery or Work?" (1999), Jennifer Cotter astutely notes how material differences between men and women are ignored in the sex work literature. Similar to Law, Kempadoo examines the process of Western women traveling to the Caribbean seeking sexual relationships with men. In this case, because of the reversal of gender relations, Kempadoo views this situation as an example of women's agency and empowerment. For Cotter, this myopic focus on agency "erases the crucial difference between those women who have access to the material resources to participate as consuming tourists in the global sex trade, and those men and women who are denied access to material resources and therefore must subordinate their 'needs' to the 'desires' of the wealthy" (2001, 7). The same criticism could be applied to Law's discussion of Philippine sex tourism, where she chides those who highlight systemic forms of inequality for reproducing "dualisms" while ignoring the material realities that position Western men on one side of the go-go bar and Filipino women on the other.

Highlighting the political economy, however, is not meant to displace or ignore how gendered and racialized discourses of Filipino women, stemming from an ignoble history of U.S. imperialism, work in tandem to sustain certain sectors of the "hospitality industry." The success of U.S. colonization in the Philippines, as I discussed in Chapter 1, depended upon both the economic and cultural components of the imperial project. In addition to teaching Filipinos English, the U.S.-based education system imposed on the Philippines institutionalized a deep sense of racial and cultural inferiority, resulting in what some scholars have described as the "de-Filipinization" of the population (Constantino 1975).

The effects of this are manifest in the proliferation of "mail-order marriages" between Western men and Filipino women. As scholars have noted, the prospect of marrying a white, American man and having blue-eyed, light-skinned children is an important factor to consider in any analysis of why Filipino women participate in this industry (Villapando 1989; Aguilar 1988). Recognizing this, numerous agencies "discourage their male clients from disclosing certain types of personal facts in their correspondence, including such potentially negative characteristics as being black or having physical disabilities" (Villapando 1989, 322). As part of the broader offensive Filipino feminists launched against prostitution and trafficking, the mail-order bride industry was officially outlawed in 1990 with RA 6955. Nevertheless, the practice continues to thrive under a number of euphemisms, including "pen-pal" and "correspondence" services.

I had the opportunity to discuss the mail-order bride phenomenon with Filipino feminist activist Gert Libang, spokesperson for GABRI-ELA, when I visited its Manila headquarters during a research trip. While discussing the possible reasons Filipino women enter into these marriages, Libang made clear that "we cannot discount the fact that some are real romance" (Libang 2007). However, she maintained that for "many of the women, they want to get out of poverty here in the Philippines. So, it's one of the push factors for them—marrying these foreign men whom they've just met through the web, whom they've just met once or twice, whom they've just talked to for 'hi' and 'hello'" (2007). Observing that the mail-order bride business is part of a larger migratory process that forces "Filipinas out of the country to work" Libang concluded that women's participation in the industry could not be construed as a real "choice" given the serious material constraints many faced. In this regard, her position reflects the general framework informing the bulk of Filipino women's activism around the subject. It is also a perspective that has generated a significant amount of controversy and debate among feminist researchers.

In a follow-up to her ethnographic work on Filipina domestic workers in Hong Kong, Nicole Constable's *Romance on a Global Stage* is among only a handful of analytical works produced on the issue. Departing from both popular media and feminist accounts that sensationalize mail-order marriages by "focus[ing] on women and universal female subordination" (2003, 4–5), Constable's text pays attention to the "complex render-ings of power that make simple binary oppositions—between men and women, oppressor and oppressed, East and West, agent and victim—naïve and obsolete" (2003, 63–64). Based on fieldwork and interviews of Filipino and Chinese women who became involved with American men via international pen-pal services, Constable acknowledges the complex array of social, economic, and cultural factors underpinning the desire of these women to begin a long-distance courtship. However, she quickly distances herself from these structural concerns by honing in on the individual desires and motivations of the participants. For example, in contrast to Mila Glodava and Richard Onizuka's *Mail-Order Brides* (1994), Constable rejects the "market metaphor" that suggests women are merely commodified objects "bought" and "sold" on the Internet (2003, 74). Although "introduction" agencies use photos of the women to sell their "pen-pal" services, Constable explains that this does not mean the women are objects themselves because they "can and do exert choice in submitting their names to an introduction agency and in deciding what to include in their listings" (2003, 74). Thus, she cautions against the market perspective for it cannot take into account how women and men "partake in their own commodification in western-oriented singles ads" (2003, 74).

Though Constable warns readers of the risks involved in "romanticiz-ing" agency, the importance she places on women and men's "choices" begs a number of important questions. For one, under what conditions are such "choices" being made? More importantly, why are the majority of women "advertising" on these sites from so-called developing countries while the men are typically from Western, First World nations? How are the categories of gender, race, and nation intimately related to issues of capitalism and class relations? A singular focus on the decisionmaking processes of individual men and women proves insufficient for under-standing the totality of forces involved in the maintenance of mail-order arrangements. As Libang noted earlier, those who oppose the industry are not discounting the fact that a certain percentage of these relationships are based on love and prove successful in the long term. However, these critics are drawing our attention to how historical, cultural, and socioeconomic factors circumscribe the "choices" made by those living in neocolonized countries like the Philippines.

In her essay "Internationalization of Capital and the Trade in Asian Women," Hsiao-Chuan Hsia offers an important counterpoint to the reigning feminist theoretical paradigm espoused by Constable and others. Locating "commodified transnational marriages within a larger, international politico-economic structure [while simultaneously analyzing] how actors within the structure search for solutions and react and interpret their surroundings," Hsia demonstrates that materialist analyses do not necessarily preclude attention to the agency of individual women and men (2004, 187). Drawing on fieldwork and interviews conducted with women from Vietnam, the Philippines, Thailand, and Cambodia, Hsia's long-term study reveals that mail-order marriages are a direct consequence of unequal capitalist development primarily between core and peripheral countries. Illustrating how austerity measures imposed by the IMF and the WB have led to the maldevelopment of countries located in the global South, Hsia exposes the gendered impact these development schemes have had on women. With limited options, migrating overseas to work or becoming a "foreign bride" is among the principal avenues many women are forced to take. Indeed, according to the data culled from her interviews, most women "expressed the hardship back home as the primary reason for their decision.... Even the few foreign brides with better-off family backgrounds also pointed out that under the unstable economic and political conditions in their home countries life is unpredictable and that they therefore hoped to find a better and more stable life for their children by marrying abroad" (2004, 216).

Explaining that these arrangements "are people's solutions to problems resulting from capital internationalization and labor liberalization," Hsia concludes that "transnational marriages crystallize an unequal international division of labor into personal relationships" (2004, 225). In contrast to Constable, who argues against accounts that depict women marrying out of "economic desperation" on the grounds that these reflect a "highly problematic orientalist, essentialist, and universalizing feminist approach [that] makes false assumptions about the determining role of material factors and political economy" (2003, 88), Hsia presents a cogent analysis that is mindful of both the "macro" and "local" aspects of mail-order marriages.

The refusal to engage in a serious discussion that situates sex tourism, the mail-order bride industry, and other facets of the sex trade within the larger international division of labor, as evidenced in the work of Law and Constable, not only neutralizes important differences among groups of people, but also has the effect of both reinforcing and naturalizing neo-liberal capitalist processes responsible for the maintenance of material differences between those in the First and the Third World. This is why the engagement between feminism and postmodernism raises important questions regarding feminism's viability as a force for radical, social transformation. As Teresa Ebert explains, the "indeterminacy that it posits as a mark of freedom and resistance is, in actuality, a legitimization of the class politics of an upper-middle class Euroamerican feminism obsessed with the freedom of the entrepreneurial subject" (1996, 30). Carol Stabile echoes this concern when she describes postmodernism as "critical theories that rely upon an uncritical and idealistic focus on the discursive constitution of the 'real,' a positivistic approach to the notion of 'difference' (one that does not consider the divisiveness of such differences), and a marked lack of critical attention to the context of capitalism and academics' location within capitalist processes of production and reproduction" (1997, 396).

When assessing the body of literature that has emerged concerning the issue of prostitution and sex work, one cannot help but notice how much contemporary feminist thought protects, rather than disrupts, the dictates of neoliberal capitalist relations. The unwillingness among certain feminist practitioners to "take a stand" on this particular issue while critiquing those who do creates a state of theoretical inertia in which these same practitioners are satisfied with analyzing issues within, rather than transforming, the existing social order. This, as Cotter argues, makes it possible to "'advance feminism' without questioning the ruling class desire to exploit those who have been positioned as 'racial' and 'sexual' others" (2001, 7).

A recent outcome of this particular theoretical position has been the scholarship produced by feminist analysts critiquing both the ideology and deployment of the term "trafficking" by some grassroots feminist NGOs to advance legislative efforts at the international and national levels. Although the definition of trafficking has expanded in the twenty-first century to include different forms of labor migration patterns in addition to prostitution, some scholars suggest that members constituting the "antitrafficking" bloc continue to craft policy that gives primacy to "prostitution" in the trafficking debates. In doing so, according to critics, antitrafficking feminist NGOs conflate prostitution with trafficking to further their own "abolitionist" efforts regarding the practice while refusing to recognize sex work as another facet of labor migration (Kempadoo and Doezema 1998; Kempadoo 2005; Ditmore 2005; Agustin 2007; Doezema 2010). Likening this position to the "moral panic" over the white slave trade that occurred during the nineteenth century, sex work advocates argue that the myopic perspective of today's "abolitionist" feminists has resulted in alliances with conservative, evangelical groups and an increasingly militarized, punitive state apparatus that utilizes antitrafficking legislation to further criminalize labor migrants from the global South (Kempadoo 2005; Ditmore 2005; Doezema 2010; Bernstein 2010). For Kempadoo, such legislation "signal[s] a growing panic at the turn of the century by the international political community and national governments about unregulated migration flows and profitable cross-border activities that lie outside state control" (2005, xiv). As a result, antitrafficking laws end up doing more harm than good because many migrants are "treated as illegal immigrants and criminals, and as threats to national security" (2005, xv). Advancing this logic, Elizabeth Bernstein writes that feminists involved in crafting antitrafficking policy promote both a "carceral feminism" and a "militarized humanitarianism" that are grounded by a punitive, neoliberal engagement with the nation-state (2010, 47).

In contrast to an earlier feminist commitment to redistributive justice, antitrafficking feminists have allegedly joined "forces with a neo-liberal project of social control … where pimps can now be given ninety-nine year prison sentences as sex traffickers and sex workers are increasingly arrested and deported for the sake of their 'protection'" (2010, 47, 57). The punitive nature of such policymaking is likely to continue in the future, according to Bernstein, given that sex trafficking is an issue that can be used by the state to "advance a larger set of geopolitical interests (be it border control, waging war, or policing the domestic underclass) [and] likely to gain traction in the broader public sphere" (2010, 67).

Even though I agree that feminists should be vigilant in ensuring that migrant women are not further criminalized by antitrafficking initiatives, I question the wisdom of eradicating or abolishing the term "trafficking" altogether, as proposed by some sex work advocates.

In an early articulation of this perspective, Alison Murray's essay "Debt Bondage and Trafficking" takes aim at the CATW, arguing that it manipulates people's feelings by "linking all forms of the sex trade together beneath an emphasis on emotive words like 'trafficking,' 'slavery,' and 'child prostitution'" (1998, 52; Lacsamana 2004). This perspective, according to Murray, is directly at odds with the "postmodern challenge to conventional feminism, which allows for the cacophony of voices and refuses the binary dichotomy in which all women are constituted as 'other'" (1998, 52; Lacsamana 2004). Given that the CATW–Asia Pacific is headquartered in Manila, and that the majority of Filipino feminist organizations prefer the term "trafficking," one could assume that Murray would perceive these organizations as belonging to the branch of feminism that fails to "overcome the binary oppositions [and] ends up supporting the status quo, impoverishing women and aligning with right-wing fundamentalism" (1998, 52).

Melissa Ditmore makes a similar critique in her assessment of the "negotiating process" by feminist NGOs involved with the UN Optional Protocol on Trafficking. Based on her own observations and participation in this policymaking procedure, Ditmore examines the divisions between two lobbying blocs: the International Human Rights Group (aligned with the Global Alliance Against Traffic in Women) and the Human Rights Network (aligned with the CATW). Whereas the former wished to distance sex work from trafficking, the latter wanted prostitution and other aspects of the sex trade to be included in the definition of trafficking in persons.

Citing the Philippine delegation's proposed definition of trafficking, which partially read "with or without consent of the victim by legal or illegal means, for all purposes of sexual exploitation including prostitution, marriage, and employment," as a representative example of the abolitionist perspective, Ditmore argues that such an "extreme" and "ludicrous" example reveals the "dangers of an obsessive and myopic focus on prostitution that it opens the door to the willing sacrifice of other essential liberties and rights in the name of eradicating prostitution" (2005, 115).

For Ditmore, some of these "essential liberties and rights" concern marriage and employment. In light of the neocolonial context of the Philippines and the proliferation and institutionalization of labor migration and the mail-order bride industry, it does not seem unreasonable that Filipino feminists sought to get this included in the definition. Specifically, their inclusion of marriage and employment reflects a broader understanding of the iniquitous power relationships between and among countries that give women certain essential liberties and rights while denying them to others. Why are the majority of mail-order brides from the Philippines? Why do Filipinos constitute one of the largest populations of international labor migrants? Answering these questions requires a framework that emphasizes how U.S. imperialism and global capitalism work in tandem to ensure the ongoing dispossession of Filipinos from their land, their livelihoods, their families, and their country. Again, I do not wish to imply that all forms of migration are entirely *forced*, but I do want to call attention to the historical, structural conditions governing the Philippines that inform and underpin the "choices" and "freedoms" women "enjoy." By discounting the Philippine delegation's position, Ditmore obscures the concrete historical processes borne out of Spanish and U.S. colonialism that are responsible for shaping specific gender ideologies of Philippine womanhood, as well as for the ongoing maldevelopment of the Philippine economy. If the strategies of the delegates were placed in a broader historical context, we might better understand why they deliberately staked out this particular position on trafficking.

For example, in a related examination of Filipino feminist efforts to enact antitrafficking legislation, Mina Roces explores how the mainstream Philippine women's movement utilized a "double narrative" of victimization and activism in their construction of "the Filipino woman" to secure passage of the Anti-Trafficking Act of 2003 (2009, 270). Acknowledging that not all Filipino feminists are united on the issue of prostitution and trafficking, Roces focuses on the dominant antitrafficking narrative that perceives prostitution as violence against women (VAW). Confronted by the vestiges of religious and colonial ideologies responsible for constructing the Filipino woman as "martyr," Filipino feminist activists, contends Roces, deployed the double narrative as a strategic measure to avoid reifying the martyr/victim ideology that has historically informed traditional views of Filipino women. She explains that if they "were going to argue that prostitution was VAW, they could deploy the victim narrative as a strategy for legislative changes to argue for the decriminalization of Filipino prostitutes [even though] the endorsement of the victim narrative was anathema to their overall campaign to fashion a new iconic woman as activist and agent" (2009, 272).

To avoid this pitfall, Filipino feminist organizations encouraged the women they were working with to become active in the broader women's movement by telling their own stories and advocating for personal empowerment (2009, 277). Although the use of the victim narrative was useful in creating practical legislative change, Roces questions the efficacy of the strategy, arguing that in certain instances it "elided" women's individual choice and agency by focusing on patriarchal and material concerns. Nonetheless, she concludes that "Filipino feminists succeeded in empowering the 'victim' without requiring the women to be 'ideal victims' that is; *only* those who were abducted or duped could be victims" (2009, 278). In the end, the passage of the Anti-Trafficking Act should be considered a victory for the Philippine women's movement. Despite some observers' skepticism toward the definition of trafficking advanced by the Philippines, specifically the insistence that trafficking occurs "with or without the victim's consent," Roces effectively illustrates how this decision "absolved the prostitutes [and] criminalized the perpetuators," thereby paving the way for women to be transformed from "victims" to "survivors" to activists (2009, 276–277).

I recognize that scholars and advocates associated with the sex work camp often consider such a position to be conservative because it undermines women's "autonomy" by advancing an allegedly "paternalistic" form of feminism premised upon viewing women as victims rather than rational agents in charge of their own economic destiny. To illustrate, in discussing CATW, Laura Agustin argues that feminist projects that view prostitution primarily as "violence against women" end up "eliminating any notion that women who sell sex can consent" (2007, 39). Moreover, when the VAW frame is used, Agustin asserts, women "become passive receptacles and mute sufferers who must be saved…. The 'trafficking' discourse relies on the notion that poorer women are better off staying at home than leaving and possibly getting into trouble" (2007, 39). In the anthology *Trafficking and Prostitution Reconsidered,* Kempadoo makes a similar claim when she states that the continued reliance on "'victim' in anti-trafficking work ... privileg[es] external forces in the conceptualization of the trafficked person, and den[ies] women's agency and subjectivity in the process" (2005, xxiii). Though Jo Doezema recognizes the importance of structural issues surrounding prostitution and sex work, she believes that "what is missing in these accounts is a critical examination of the power involved in producing knowledge about 'trafficking in women' and the ways in which dominant constructions of the issue emerge and are incorporated into policy, [specifically] the relationships among those who shape meanings of 'trafficking in women' and between these 'discourse masters' and the objects of their concern: the 'sex slaves'" (2010, 11). What I find mystifying about these analytical formulations is their focus on individual, rather than collective, forms of resistance.

In relation to the Philippines and Roces's concept of the double narrative, we can see clearly that members of Filipino women's organizations were responsible for articulating both a macro- and microperspective that generated respect for the women they worked with. Indeed, the effort to provide the necessary supports and tools that enable women to become active participants in various feminist organizations "reveals the genuine desire for women's movements to have a mass following while legitimizing their organization's claim to 'speak' for prostitutes" (2009, 279). This strategy, I argue, has been one of the reasons that the Philippine women's movement remains one of the most vibrant and politically active in the world. A related example of collective resistance is the organization AMMORE (Action Network for Marriage, Migrants' Rights, and Empowerment), which was founded shortly after the 2007 International Conference on Border Control and Empowerment for Immigrant Brides and includes migrant workers from the Philippines, Vietnam, Japan, Taiwan, and South Korea, among others. Challenging those that assume "efforts to prevent 'trafficking' often try to prevent migration itself" (Agustin 2007, 40), members of AMMORE distribute pamphlets that state, "We are migrants. We are workers. We are people with rights and dignity" (AMMORE brochure). Although AMMORE members make clear that "poverty, intensified by the neo-liberal globalization agenda, has put women from underdeveloped and developing countries in situations vulnerable to abuse and exploitation by marriage bureaus and matchmaking agencies," they are not passive victims or mute sufferers, as much of the recent feminist literature would have us believe. AMMORE's emphasis on strengthening "the organized ranks of grassroots marriage migrants" through education, advocacy, and organizing (AMMORE brochure) belies the sex work position that such a perspective robs women of their agentive capacities.

Attention to the micropolitics of power and to discursive regimes that supposedly discipline women's bodies is a common template in the field of feminist thought. At this juncture, one could argue that there are two competing "discourse masters" at work in these debates: that of the grassroots activists involved with NGOs that lobby for regulation and attention to the situation of women involved in the sex industry and that of the postmodern-influenced feminist theorists who argue for greater "autonomy" and "freedom" for women within existing capitalist relations. As Cotter points out, however, the "'freedom' to 'choose' sex work (which itself presupposes a class society) is only the highly restricted and formal 'freedom' that capitalism has always allowed its workers: freedom from property and the freedom to sell one's own labor-power. In short, it is the 'freedom' to be exploited in the way one 'chooses' but not the freedom from exploitation" (2001, 7).

Returning to my earlier essay (2004) on the subject, I want to venture a step further by applying Bridget Anderson's cogent analysis of domestic work to the issue of prostitution. As I previously discussed in Chapter 3, Anderson argues that a domestic worker is selling her "personhood" rather than her labor power as a result of the "caring function" of domestic work (2000, 2–3). This challenges the emotional labor paradigm espoused by Wendy Chapkis and other advocates of the sex work position; for both the prostitute and the domestic worker there is no real separation between the public and private because "they are defined in a very real sense by their social relations, characterized by personal dependency on the employer" (Anderson 2000, 4). Unfortunately, in our "postmodern condition," scholars and activists who give primacy to material and external conditions are summarily dismissed as "determinists" by the postmodernist discourse master in much the same way grassroots abolitionist NGOs are chastised for their activism around trafficking and prostitution.

Despite the ongoing debates around trafficking in feminist theory, one cannot deny the innumerable accomplishments Filipino women have made on this particular issue. Their grassroots activism serves as a counterpoint to the apolitical, conservative brand of theorizing that refuses to imagine an alternative social order. In addition to the Anti-Trafficking Act of 2003, their efforts to organize around issues of militarized rape and prostitution have proved transformative, as evidenced by the much publicized and historic 2005 Subic rape case, which is discussed in the next chapter.

Chapter Five

✦

Empire on Trial

The Subic Rape Case and the Struggle for Philippine Women's Liberation

It wasn't easy for me to file a complaint against my rapists. And neither was the (legal) system kind to me after I decided to pursue the case. Instead of taking my side in the fight, our government took steps to make my situation much harder. I have not received a single message of support from our woman President, while the secretary of justice has even repeatedly defended my rapists.

—*Nicole, November 1, 2006,*
"Nicole's Ordeal Is More Than Rape"

My conscience continues to bother me realizing that I may have in fact been so friendly and intimate with Daniel Smith at the Neptune Club that he was led to believe that I was amenable to having sex or that we simply just got carried away. I would rather risk public outrage than do nothing to help the court in ensuring that justice is served.

—*Nicole, March 12, 2009,*
"My Conscience Bothered Me"

By the time Philippine media outlets were alerted to the March 12, 2009, affidavit signaling that Nicole, the pseudonym of the woman at the center of the Subic rape case, had "recanted" her earlier testimony accusing U.S. Marine Daniel Smith of raping her almost four years earlier, she had already fired her lawyer, Evalyn Ursua; accepted a settlement from the accused; and departed for the United States, where she planned to live permanently. This was a stunning decision in an epic legal battle that, less than three years earlier, had resulted in the historic conviction of Smith for the rape of Nicole on November 1, 2005, marking the first time a member of the U.S. military had ever been tried, convicted, and sentenced for a crime on Philippine soil. For many Filipinos, the landmark "guilty" verdict and the sentencing of Smith to forty years in a Philippine penitentiary delivered by Makati regional trial judge Benjamin Pozon on December 4, 2006, represented not only a victory for Nicole but also for a nation that had grown accustomed to seeing its own interests subordinated to those of its former colonial ruler. The victory, unfortunately, would be short-lived: On the evening of December 29, 2006, Smith was secretly transferred from the Makati City Jail to the U.S. Embassy to await his appeal, once more throwing the issue of Philippine sovereignty starkly into question.

In addition to highlighting critical questions concerning violence against women and sexual assault, the Subic rape case has reignited protests over U.S. military intervention in the Philippines, specifically regarding the terms and conditions outlined in the controversial Visiting Forces Agreement. Seven years after a broad coalition of progressive forces had successfully ousted the two major U.S. military installations, Subic Bay Naval Base (Olongapo City) and Clark Air Force Base (Angles City), President Joseph Estrada signed the VFA into law in 1998, granting the U.S. military *unlimited* access to twenty-two ports throughout the country to conduct "joint" training exercises with members of the Armed Forces of the Philippines. Deployments of U.S. troops has escalated since the 9/11 attacks and the war on terror, with the majority of soldiers being sent to the southern, predominately Muslim region of the country. Though the stated goal of their mission is to provide humanitarian aid to the war-torn area, most believe U.S. military personnel are involved in a counterterrorist operation against the Abu-Sayyaf.

As well as enabling the U.S. military to reestablish a dominant presence throughout the archipelago, the VFA extends extraordinary privileges and protections to U.S. soldiers, effectively undermining the sovereignty of the Philippines and, by extension, the safety and dignity of its citizens. For example, Article III, "Entry and Departure," of the VFA states that members of the U.S. military are "exempt from passport and visa regulations upon entering and departing the Philippines." Article IV, "Driving and Vehicle Registration," stipulates that Philippine officials will "acccpt as valid, without test or fee, a driving permit or license issued by the appropriate United States personnel for the operation of military or official vehicles" and that U.S. government vehicles "need not be registered, but shall have appropriate markings." Moreover, Article VII, "Importation and Exportation," excuses U.S. soldiers from paying taxes and duty fees on items purchased during their "temporary stay" in the Philippines (Visiting Forces Agreement 1998).

The most flagrant violation of Philippine sovereignty, however, is found under Article V, "Criminal Jurisdiction." In the case of crimes committed by members of the U.S. armed forces, "Philippine authorities will, upon request by the United States, waive their primary right to exercise jurisdiction except in cases of particular importance to the Philippines" (Visiting Forces Agreement 1998). If the Philippine government decides not to waive its right, officials have twenty days, after receiving the U.S. request, to submit their communication to U.S. authorities. Should the Philippines be granted the right to prosecute a U.S. soldier for a criminal offense, Article V requires all legal proceedings to be completed within a one-year period, during which the accused will remain in the custody of the U.S. military. If a soldier is convicted, the U.S. government has an unspecified amount of time to appeal.

In contrast, the complementary agreement governing the treatment of visiting Filipino soldiers to the United States, known as the VFA 2, requires that they be detained in a U.S. jail. Specifically, Article 9 states that if a Filipino serviceman is accused of committing a crime in the U.S., "confinement imposed by a United States federal or state court upon a Republic of the Philippines personnel shall be served in penal institutions in the United States suitable for the custody level of the prisoners, chosen after consultation between the two governments." This provision once more illustrates the inherent inequities underpinning the military arrangements (Uy and Guinto 2009).

Long before Nicole brought charges against her accused rapists, the lopsided provisions contained within the VFA raised alarm for Filipino feminists. Days after Ramos signed the treaty, GABRIELA argued that the VFA, specifically Article V, provided U.S. military personnel with the "diplomatic license to violate our women and children" (GABRIELA 1998). The organization's concerns were not unfounded; incidences of sexual assault perpetrated by U.S. servicemen against Filipino women had become routine around the military bases. During the Marcos dictatorship, for example, a U.S. soldier was allowed to leave the country after it was discovered he was responsible for organizing a prostitution ring in Olongapo involving twelve young girls, otherwise known as the Olongapo Twelve, infected with a number of sexually transmitted diseases (San Juan 1998). In another case, a U.S. soldier escaped prosecution for the rape and murder of Rosario Baluyot, a twelve-year-old girl who died after being poisoned by a vibrator that had been broken off and left inside her body.

Though gruesome, both of these crimes belong to a much larger pattern of militarized violence, comprising approximately 2,000 reported cases in the post–World War II period that never reached Philippine courts (Rosca 2007, 2). Susan R. McKay reminds us that these patterns of gendered violence are typically manifest indirectly, through macroforces, such as the global economy or international law, and directly through interpersonal forms of violence, such as assault and rape. However, McKay claims "it is essential that both indirect and direct violence toward women are understood as fundamental phenomena that maintain inequality" (1998, 349). This is why, in the shadow of the U.S. military and the VFA, the Subic rape case takes on a special significance when connected to structural and microforms of violence against women in militarized spaces.

After a night of drinking at the Neptune Club in Subic Freeport, home to the former naval base, a U.S. Marine raped Nicole inside a moving van as three of his friends cheered him on. Afterward, Nicole was dumped, half-clothed, on the side of the road as the van sped off. Court documents later identified the accused as Lance Corporals Daniel Smith, Keith Silkwood, and Dominic Duplantis and Staff Sergeant Chad Carpenter.

Members of the Thirty-first Marine Expeditionary Force stationed in Okinawa, the four soldiers had just completed *Balikatan* exercises with members of the Philippine military. Adhering to the guidelines of the VFA, a one-year deadline was imposed for the trial, thus placing the prosecution team under enormous pressure to present its case with the necessary evidence. It quickly became clear that Nicole was not simply going to trial against four soldiers; a military superpower was prepared to flex its political and economic muscle to protect its personnel from prosecution.

During the proceedings, Duplantis, Carpentier, and Silkwood maintained their innocence by corroborating Smith's testimony that he and the victim engaged in "consensual sex." Although these three soldiers were eventually acquitted for lack of evidence, the conviction of Smith rested on DNA evidence and Judge Pozon's interpretation of RA 8353, otherwise known as the Anti-Rape Law of 1997 (Republic of the Philippines 1997). Testimony from medical experts, bar patrons, and police investigators indicated that "Nicole" was too intoxicated to "consent" to sex with Smith. Agreeing with their findings, Pozon delivered the landmark "guilty" verdict, sentencing Smith to forty years in the Makati City Jail and ordering him to pay "Nicole" P100,000 ($2,000). In the lengthy decision Pozon argued the "court is morally convinced that Smith committed the crime charged. He admitted having sex with the complainant whom he knew was intoxicated.... Thus she could not have consented on the bestial acts of the accused" (Torres 2006). According to the Anti-Rape Law a rape is committed "when the offended party is deprived of reason or otherwise unconscious" (Republic of the Philippines 1997). After the verdict, Smith was escorted directly to the Makati City Jail to begin his sentence, despite appeals from his lawyers to have him remain in U.S. custody.

Outraged over the conviction, the United States threatened to cancel all future joint military exercises if Smith was not transferred back to the U.S. Embassy to appeal the decision. With the AFP having "received the most dramatic increase in foreign military funding from the U.S. since 2001" (Docena 2006), the prospect of losing a critical source of financial support proved too great for the Arroyo administration. Circumventing Pozon's decision, an agreement was signed between Foreign Affairs secretary Alberto Romulo and U.S. ambassador to the Philippines Kristie

Kenney enabling Smith's return to the U.S. Embassy after his having served only twenty-five days of his sentence. Soon after, the resumption of *Balikatan* operations was announced, and the U.S. Marines issued a public statement promising that its members would commit "no more rape" during their stay in the Philippines (Orejas 2007).

The diplomatic bullying and behind-the-scenes legal wrangling that U.S. officials used to secure Smith's custody underscore the neocolonial relationship between the United States and the Philippines. This is most evident when compared to the way U.S. officials have recently handled other high-profile military crimes in the region. For example, in 2007 the U.S. Army publicly apologized to South Korean officials for the rape of a sixty-seven-year-old woman by a U.S. solider, claiming that the "vicious act is an affront to all soldiers" and assuring the country that the U.S. military was "cooperating fully with Korean authorities" (Agence France-Presse 2007). A similar situation occurred in 2008 after Japanese authorities detained a U.S. Marine for the abduction and alleged rape of a fourteen-year-old young woman. Although she dropped the charges a few days later, the U.S. Marine Corps conducted its own internal investigation and sentenced the man to four years in prison for "abusive sexual conduct with a Japanese teenager in Okinawa" (Wright 2008, 3). Fearing the incident would endanger the important military alliance between the two countries, U.S. officials, including Secretary of State Condoleeza Rice, issued formal apologies to Prime Minister Yasuo Fukuda and Foreign Minister Mashiko Komura (Wright 2008, 2). Reminiscent of the widely publicized 1995 Okinawan rape case, which involved the prosecution and sentencing of three U.S. soldiers to seven years in a Japanese penitentiary for the gang rape of a twelve-year-old Okinawan schoolgirl, the effort made by U.S. authorities to smooth over diplomatic relations stands in sharp contrast to their handling of the Subic rape case.

By highlighting these recent events, however, I am not implying that the United States is, or has always been, cooperative with governments hosting its military installations. Rather, these transnational comparisons reveal similarities and differences across regions. Barbara Sutton and Julie Novkov stress the importance of exposing "'linkages' among different places, underscoring how social processes and ideologies in one area of the world relate to crises, power struggles, or political designs in other areas" (2008, 11). Similarly to Filipinos, South Koreans and Okinawans have all seen their sovereignty jeopardized by status of forces agreements (SOFAs) that govern the behavior of U.S. military personnel during their tours of duty. Typically, SOFAs are negotiated in private between the U.S. government and the specific country that will be "home" to its military base (Moon 1997; Enloe 2000). As a result, the United States has frequently invoked the shield of these military agreements to protect its troops from prosecution for crimes such as rape and/or murder. For example, in Okinawa "between 1972 and 1995, U.S. servicemen were implicated in 4,716 crimes, nearly one per day ... and few indeed have suffered any inconvenience for their crimes" (Magdoff et al. 2002, 9). On the rare occasion that a serviceman is actually punished for a crime in the "host" country, it is largely due to organized antibases protests, particularly those spearheaded by grassroots women's organizations that draw explicit attention to the gendered and racialized dimensions of military violence.

Cynthia Enloe explains that during the 1970s, after a string of unsolved murders allegedly perpetrated by U.S. soldiers, South Korean women located in and around the military camp towns began organizing and pressuring the local police and government officials to be more vigilant in tracking down the assailants (2000, 92). Similarly, in the aftermath of the 1995 gang rape in Okinawa, Japanese women forged broad coalitions with South Korean and Filipino feminists to protest U.S. militarization throughout the Asia Pacific region. In the Philippines, the women's movement has a lengthy history of utilizing rallies, vigils, marches, and other forms of public protest to demonstrate their opposition to U.S. military aggression, acknowledging that the presence of U.S. troops is "more than a question of sovereignty [but] is in fact a question of national dignity, class inequalities, sexual politics, and racism" (Santos 1992, 38). Expanding the anti-imperialist nationalist movement's analysis of militarization to include issues of gender and race, the Philippine women's movement makes explicit that national liberation is intimately tied to women's liberation. By directing assailing U.S. militarism, and by extension U.S. imperialism, Filipino women's grassroots activism underscores the importance and necessity of a "nationalist feminist" perspective in a Third World formation. Despite the fact that nationalism has been maligned in much of Western feminist theory because of its modernist and patriarchal moorings, Filipino feminists, through vigorous debate and dialogue with their male counterparts, have forged a unique and vibrant anti-imperialist women's liberation movement. As Filipino critic Delia Aguilar notes, many Filipino women strongly believe that "freedom from oppression as women can become possible only when the nation is liberated from U.S. domination and when the majority of the people can be released from poverty, illness, malnutrition, and other forms of deprivation rampant in a neocolony" (1998, 45). Thus, it makes sense that a focal point for women's organizing would center on the effects of U.S. militarism in the country, symbolic of both the suppression of Philippine sovereignty and the violation of Filipino women's dignity.

Prior to granting formal independence to the Philippines on July 4, 1946, the United States signed the Military Bases Agreement and the Military Assistance Agreement enabling it to maintain two major military installations in the Philippines—Clark Air Force Base and Subic Naval Base—along with twenty-three smaller facilities. Often praised by both U.S. and Philippine governments for providing an economic boost to the country, the military facilities became notorious for generating prostitution in their respective communities. According to the feminist NGO the Women's Education, Development, Productivity, and Research Organization (WeDpro), 70 percent of women working around the bases "were in prostitution well before they turned 18," with 50 percent reporting they had "never worked in similar situations" prior to working in the "entertainment" or "red light" districts (Santos, Hofmann, and Bulawan 1998, 3). The sheer magnitude of prostitution during this period resulted in its "normalization" whereby the sexual assault and exploitation of women became a routine, acceptable part of life in the cities of Angles and Olongapo (1998, 3). Not surprisingly, the presence of the bases further inculcated a deep sense of racial and cultural inferiority among many Filipinos, particularly women, who often found themselves attempting to reconcile contradictory processes where "redemptive hopes and expectations—through love and marriage, escape to the United States and its glories—violently collid[ed] with the environs in which these are nurtured, suffused as the bases [were] by naked exploitation" (Aguilar 1998, 7). As a result of these unequal conditions, most women were left behind to care for the thousands of Amerasian children abandoned by servicemen once their stay in the Philippines had expired. According to Gwyn Kirk and Margo Okazawa-Rey, the situation for these children had become so acute that a lawsuit was filed in the United States in 1993 on their behalf, although it was not "considered in any serious way" by U.S. government officials (1998, 312).

Throughout the 1980s, various sectors of the Philippine women's movement, including GABRIELA, the BUKLOD Center, the Coalition Against Trafficking in Women–Asia Pacific, and WeDpro, mobilized to respond to the crisis of militarized prostitution by creating women's shelters, providing health and counseling services, and giving educational seminars on HIV/AIDS, among other practical initiatives (Santos, Hofmann, and Bulawan 1998; Kirk and Okazawa-Rey 1998). Together, in conjunction with the broader anti-imperialist nationalist movement, Filipino feminists played an important role in convincing members of the Philippine Senate to reject the lease renewal on the bases in 1991. Preferring the term "prostituted women" to connote the larger socioeconomic factors responsible for forcing many women into the industry, Filipino feminist activists have been vocal in their efforts to end the traffic in women and children.

As demonstrated in the previous chapter, this antitrafficking position has, in certain feminist theoretical circles, provoked consternation among those who claim such efforts do more harm than good to the women involved. For example, in her analysis of Korean NGOs involved in antitrafficking campaigns, Na Young Lee acknowledges the significant accomplishments of various groups in bringing greater attention to issues of militarism and prostitution, but she nevertheless argues that they "cannot allow any other perspectives besides the anti-sex work feminist position which sees prostitution as a form of sexual exploitation or patriarchal crimes" (2006, 465). According to Lee, by using terms such as "prostituted women" instead of "sex workers," these NGOs obscure the diversity and complexity of women's individual lives when there is an "official frame or master narrative informing a particular analysis" (2006, 466).

In many ways, Lee's work echoes that of Anne-Marie Hilsdon, who, in one of the only scholarly accounts of gender and militarism in the Philippines, argues that "prostitution at the former US bases was a narrative of both exploitation and agency" because it allowed greater economic and sexual independence for Filipino women compared to those living in more rural areas (1995, 106). The social costs of such independence, however, are rarely discussed in analytical formulations dedicated to recuperating women's agency at the expense of other pressing considerations.

Indeed, this specific theoretical stance has grown in popularity over the recent years as feminists have become increasingly more interested in examining women's subjectivity within the libidinal, rather than the political, economy.

As useful as these accounts may be for delving into the minutiae of individual women's lives, they fail to imagine alternatives to the exist ing social order, constrained, as they are, by ideological requirements to dispense with the material or "official frame" in favor of obfuscatory discursive analyses that do little to destabilize the economic, social, or political forces underpinning the exploitation of Third World women's labor and sexuality. To illustrate, in her deployment of a Foucauldian lens to analyze militarized gender violence, Hilsdon's scholarship focuses on the "positioning of women" in the "confrontation between liberation and state armies—that is the Communist Party of the Philippines/New People's Army (CPP/NPA) and the ... Armed Forces of the Philippines (AFP)" (1995, 2). Adhering to Michel Foucault's famous dictum that power is "capillary," Hilsdon effectively levels the important distinctions between the AFP and NPA by arguing that neither the "state nor its army has a monopoly on disciplinary power" (1995, 25). This revelation might come as a shock to the numerous Filipinos who have been unjustly subjected to intensified government harassment and state military intimi-dation since the election of President Gloria Macapagal-Arroyo in 2001, who continued the all-out war against the Philippine Left initiated by her predecessors. Against this volatile backdrop of contemporary Philip-pine life, Hilsdon's scholarship can serve as a cautionary tale, exposing the pitfalls and limitations of postmodern politics. In contrast, the anti-imperialist feminist perspective informing grassroots Filipino women's activism against U.S. militarism can serve as a necessary antidote to the recent spate of postmodern-inspired feminist theoretical production. By organizing mass campaigns against militarized sexual violence, the Phil-ippine women's movement has helped raise the profile of a historically overlooked by-product of U.S.-Philippine relations, arguably paving the way for the historic conviction of Daniel Smith in 2005.

United under the slogan "Justice for Nicole, Justice for Our Nation," members of GABRIELA, Task Force Subic Rape, and the Nicole In-formation Bureau worked collectively throughout the court proceedings to monitor the trial, provide support to Nicole and her family, and help educate the general public about the relationship of the case to the larger issue of Philippine sovereignty. (GABRIELA has played a critical role during its history in advocating on behalf of women who have suffered under unjust military agreements.) In the aftermath of the Subic rape, women affiliated with GABRIELA continued to pressure the Arroyo administration to nullify the VFA, "claiming the government is putting more weight to the apparent success of the U.S.-backed campaign against the Abu-Sayyaf to stifle calls for the review or scrapping of the RP-US Visiting Forces Agreement" (Alipala 2007). Other groups, such as TFSR, a women-led coalition of seventeen member organizations working outside the purview of GABRIELA, were created to "support a fair trial for Nicole's case and to bring justice not only to Nicole, but also to the women and children violated by the U.S.-led wars of aggression all over the world" (Task Force Subic Rape 2006, 8). Members drafted and distributed a primer on the Anti-Rape Law of 1997 and the VFA and encouraged citizens to "always anchor the rape case on the issue of the legitimacy of the VFA and how this agreement violates the sovereignty of the Philippines as a duly recognized independent state" (2006, 7). Similarly, the Nicole Defense Campaign and its media relations arm, the Nicole Information Bureau, developed online resources to provide the public inside and outside the Philippines with accurate information concerning the trial. For example, a paper outlining the specific connections between the Subic rape case and the VFA is contained on their Web site, among various other documents. Specifically, the paper explains that, even though the VFA is a variation of the SOFA that the United States has in place with other countries hosting its military installations, the VFA is significantly different because it was negotiated in the absence of bases, therefore placing the *entire* country under the auspices of its terms and regulations (www.subicrapecase.wordpress.com). Because this agreement essentially gives the U.S. military unchecked power over the whole territory of the Philippines, the vigorous, organized response of a diverse array of Filipino feminists is evidence of the tremendous importance placed on the outcome of the Subic rape case.

Given this context, many of Nicole's supporters were shocked and saddened when her second affidavit emerged. Nevertheless, they urged the public not to blame Nicole for her decision, acknowledging the tremendous pressure and scrutiny she and her family had faced since 2005.

Speaking on behalf of GABRIELA, Liza Maza characterized Nicole's sudden change of heart as "unfortunate," noting that it made her a "victim of three aspects: rape, the government, and the VFA" (Maragay 2009). In a statement to the press, Nicole's former lawyer, Evalyn Ursua, explained that the family had grown "tired of the case" and that Nicole had left the country because "there was no justice" in the Philippines (Jimenez-David 2009). Women's groups were also quick to counter media reports that Nicole had "recanted," arguing that she never retracted her original claim that she had been raped by Smith. On the TFSR Web site, members of the task force reminded readers that there were "three other conditions for rape apart from sexual coercion," including the victim being "drugged or intoxicated." Arguing that her "affidavit was not a recantation," TFSR reiterated Pozon's decision that Nicole was too intoxicated to give consent to Smith (www.subicrapecase.wordpress.com).

Moreover, feminist organizations stressed that the affidavit was completely irrelevant because the Anti-Rape Law of 1997 declared rape to be a *public*, rather than a private, crime. This meant that the trial, having already been determined, was no longer between Nicole and Smith but rather the Republic of the Philippines and Smith. Nevertheless, many were left puzzled by both the timing of her decision and the surreptitious manner in which her affidavit was executed. For example, just a month earlier, on February 11, 2009, the Philippine Supreme Court had ruled that Smith be returned immediately to Philippine custody. In their decision, the judges argued that the "Romulo-Kenney agreements of Dec. 19 and 22, 2006, which are agreements on the detention of the accused in the United States Embassy, are not in accord with the VFA itself because such detention is not 'by Philippine authorities'" (GMA News 2009, 2). Though the Supreme Court did not declare the VFA illegal, as many had hoped, its judgment remanding Smith to Philippine custody was, in light of the circumstances, a momentary victory for Nicole and her legal team.

Despite the ruling, however, the United States refused to hand Smith over to Philippine authorities. This blatant rejection of Philippine law only strengthened calls, among progressive nationalist organizations, to abrogate the VFA. By early March, with Smith continuing to languish in U.S. custody, newly elected U.S. president Barack Obama made a "surprise" phone call to President Arroyo assuring her of his continued support for the VFA. Two days later, Nicole signed her "recantation" in the office of the law firm representing Smith and left for the United States. In response to suggestions that Nicole might have been pressured or bribed by U.S. officials to change her previous testimony, Nicole's mother asked the public to respect her decision, noting that the family had "fought long enough. We just want peace of mind, to live quietly" (Quismundo and Alipala 2009, 2). She went on to explain that the protracted legal battle had taken a toll on her daughter, stating, "Every time we went out and people recognized us, my daughter almost melted with shame. We couldn't have peace" (2009). In discussing militarized sexual violence, Enloe explains that rape victims often have to navigate conflicting and complex emotions as they formulate a response to their assault. In most cases, these women have to weigh "their relationships to the rapists and to her personal friends and relatives, to the prevailing norms of feminine respectability, and perhaps to the criminal justice system, but *in addition,* she must weigh her relationships to collective memory, collective notions of national destiny, and the very institutions of organized violence" (2000, 111). Though it is futile to speculate on what planted the seeds of doubt in Nicole's mind, the historic circumstances surrounding her trial must be tied forever to the collective memory of the thousands of Filipinas who preceded her down the difficult and daunting task of seeking justice and accountability from the imperial hegemon.

Notwithstanding the presence of a well-organized women's movement, the Subic rape case exposed contradictions regarding traditional notions of Philippine womanhood and femininity, with some women rallying behind Smith while publicly chastising Nicole for her "reckless" behavior. In letters written to the *Philippine Daily Inquirer,* for example, some Filipinas expressed their willingness to join a "club or something in support of Smith" while others questioned Nicole's motives by asking "what kind of woman will get herself drunk in a bar, flirt with soldiers, go out with them, and expect not to get molested?" (Tulfo 2006). The release of two pornographic DVDs titled *Olongapo Scandal* and *Nicole,* both based on the events of November 1, 2005, only added to the public humiliation Nicole endured. Although it has been common in rape cases to "blame the victim," it is important to locate these responses to Nicole within the history of Spanish and U.S. colonialism.

One of the most enduring legacies of 350 years of Spanish colonial rule was the introduction of Catholicism, which radically altered existing ideologies concerning gender and sexuality. Discussing this period, Elizabeth Eviota notes that "religion was to have different consequences for women and men," thus producing a sexual double standard that circumscribed Filipino women's sexuality and relegated Filipino women to the domestic sphere (1992, 39). According to the teachings of the Catholic church, "Daughters should be taught to fear God, to take care of their virginity, and to be modest so as not to be taken advantage of by men. Women should be taught to keep house and to love the home because according to the Bible, the fortunes of the household lay on their shoulders" (1992, 60). Spanish colonialists justified the regulation of Filipino women's sexual behavior through religious doctrine because they felt most were "'licentious' and 'immoral' [and] did not know the meaning of 'love'" (1992, 41).

In her perspicacious analysis of colonial discourses in the Dutch East Indies, Ann Laura Stoler explains that "sexual promiscuity or restraint were not abstract characteristics attached to any persons who exhibited those behaviors, but as often post-hoc interpretations contingent on the racialized class and gendered categories to which individuals were already assigned" (1995, 115). By describing Filipino women as "erotically driven, sensually charged, and sexually precocious," the Spanish were able to further their colonial project through the religious disciplining of Filipino women's sexuality (Stoler 1995, 115; Eviota 1992, 39). Women who stepped outside of the traditional notions of respectable Philippine femininity were subjected to censure and rebuke. Several centuries later, the Catholic church continues to wield enormous influence in the social and political affairs of the Philippines. With over 90 percent of the population Catholic, divorce remains illegal in the country, abortion is prohibited, as is contraception, thereby limiting the availability of condoms and other methods of family planning to Filipino citizens. In this context, it is not difficult to see why Nicole and the Subic rape case stirred so many differing emotions.

Indeed, these cultural ideals governing Philippine womanhood manifested themselves a little more than a month after Nicole left the country when the Philippine Court of Appeals (CA) acquitted Lance Corporal Daniel Smith. In the court's decision, the justices, composed of three women, ruled that Smith and Nicole had shared a "spontaneous, unplanned romantic episode" and had simply been "carried away by their passions" (Torres 2009). The judgment also indicted Nicole for her "audacity" in flirting with Smith with "reckless abandon," claiming that when their brief "romance" ended, Nicole became irritated and charged Smith with rape. Despite the mounds of medical testimony presented at the original trial indicating force had been used, the CA claimed it could find "no evidence" that this was the case. Within hours of his acquittal, Smith left the country for a "secret" location to be reunited with his family, ending a nearly three-year legal battle that, if the conviction had been upheld, would have been a momentous victory for Filipino women and Philippine sovereignty. Smith's acquittal has only strengthened the resolve of the Philippine women's movement, however, as mass protests demanding the abolition of the VFA continue at the time of this writing.

CONCLUSION

The textual activism of contemporary critique is an extension of, not an opposition (or even resistance) to capitalism.
—*Teresa Ebert, The Task of Cultural Critique*

MAKIBAKA! HUWAG MATAKOT! (Struggle!
Do Not Fear! Do Not Be Afraid!)
—*Filipino rallying cry popularized during the Marcos era*

In August 2010, I traveled to Montreal, Canada, to attend the first Montreal International Women's Conference. Hosted by the March 8 Committee of Women of Diverse Origins, a grassroots, anti-imperialist women's network (wdofo.wordpress.com), the conference brought together feminist activists from the Philippines, Mali, Iran, Palestine, and Sri Lanka, among others to advance a "militant global women's movement in the 21st century" (miwc2010.wordpress.com). GABRIELA–Philippines, a co-organizer of the conference, had numerous members of its organization in attendance, including GWP president Liza Maza, who delivered the keynote address: "Moving Forward to a Women's Movement in the 21st Century" (miwc2010.wordpress.com). After discussing many of the obstacles confronting women located in the global South and North, including the worsening financial crisis, environmental degradation, landlessness, labor migration, women's reproductive health, imperialism, and militarization, she ended her lecture by repeatedly shouting, "MAKIBAKA! HUWAG MATAKOT!" (Struggle! Do Not Fear! Do Not Be Afraid!). Members of GABRIELA–Philippines and those affiliated with its chapters in the United States and Canada joined Maza by standing, fists in the air, imploring conference attendees to further the collective efforts against neoliberal imperialist policies that continue to imperil the majority of the world's population.

Energized by what I witnessed in the conference hall that morning, I began reflecting on the state of feminist theory, specifically what Marxist critic Teresa Ebert describes as the "textual activism of contemporary critique" (2009, 6). In contrast to the collective praxis, strategizing, and networking that transpired among conference participants that weekend in Montreal, hegemonic feminist thought, informed by the dictates of the cultural turn, appeared out of synch with the lived realities of many women who came to share their experiences. The most obvious difference could be found in the language, the discourse if you will, of the conference program, which included plenary sessions titled "Imperialism and Its Impact on Women," "Women's Oppression and Exploitation," and "Building Resistances," and workshops such as "Women Workers Fighting Exploitation," "Women Resisting Wars and Imperialist Aggression," and "Women's Health and Reproductive Rights," to name a few (Montreal International Women's Conference 2010 Conference Program). Here, the effects of capitalist globalization on women living and laboring in the maldeveloped South were not obscured by linguistic play emphasizing their hybrid identities or flexible citizenship or their resourcefulness as they crafted survival strategies to mitigate against some of the worst abuses they endured as migrants working as live-in caregivers and/or domestic workers. Resistance was conceived as collective, rather than individual, and the goal was to build a global network of women committed to transforming, rather than working within, existing social relations, as evidenced by the formation of the International Women's Alliance on the final day of the conference. Finally, imperialism was not perceived as "over" anymore than the nation-state was considered "dead"; one need only look at the ongoing political and military dominance of the United States, exemplified by the "global war on terror" for proof of both.

By comparing the analysis and activism of women at this conference with the "textual activism" of contemporary feminist theory, I do not intend to discredit or dismiss the importance of knowledge production in academic centers. However, as a feminist scholar and teacher, I am concerned with the direction feminist theorizing has taken over the past thirty or so years. In a recent evaluation of the discipline, Hester Eisenstein explains that in the 1960s and 1970s feminist practitioners were engaged in lively debates concerning the relationship between women's liberation and capitalist exploitation. Unfortunately, as I've discussed throughout this book, by the 1980s and the advent of the cultural turn, systemic analyses of capitalism were rendered obsolete (Eisenstein 2009, 2). Though Eisenstein suggests that feminism reengaged with capitalist politics in the 1990s with the evolution of postcolonial theory, I remain wary, arguing instead that the analytical retreat from capitalist exploitation has continued to the present day, resulting in what Ebert terms "cultural critique" (Ebert 2009). This mode of theoretical explanation derives from the cultural turn, which "becomes more prominent at times of intense class contradictions" (Ebert 2009, xv). Cultural critique utilizes "textual activism" to produce "subversive readings that give pleasure to the reader and reassure her of her discursive agency, because such agency is spectral" (2009, xv). Although "class" is liberally used in such examinations (along with capitalism and exploitation), its meaning is emptied of any explanatory power and reduced to "lifestyle" in contrast to the Marxist interpretation, in which class is understood as the "relationship of owning the labor of others (living and past) because labor is a commodity unlike any other" (2009, xiv). What results, then, is a theory that works in tandem with capitalism rather than in opposition, a reformist, rather than revolutionary, analytical position.

Throughout this book my goal has been to clearly illustrate how this mode of analysis, particularly in feminist accounts focusing on the Philippines, obfuscates and suppresses the violent, historical, and contemporary processes of U.S. imperialist policy. For example, in the lead up to the 2010 presidential elections, two events encapsulate the culture of impunity that characterized the Arroyo administration's tenure: the abduction of Filipino American activist Melissa Roxas and the Maguindanao massacre. On May 19, 2009, Melissa Roxas, who had relocated from the United States to the Philippines in 2007 to pursue human rights work, was abducted along with two companions by fifteen armed and hooded men from a house she was staying at in La Paz, Tarlac. At the time of her abduction, Roxas had been a part of a medical mission in the region.

Six days later she "surfaced" in Quezon City, after enduring days of torture, including asphyxiation, by her captors. According to her affidavit and subsequent accounts, Roxas was abducted by state military agents and held at Fort Magsaysay during her illegal detention. Throughout her interrogation, Roxas was told she had been abducted because she was suspected to be a member of the CPP and the NPA. Despite her repeated denials of this charge, Roxas was subjected to a range of torture techniques before finally being dropped off near a relative's house. Roxas returned to the United States to be with her family in California, but she traveled back to the Philippines two months later to pursue her case in the Philippine courts.

Several months later, on November 23, 2009, fifty-seven people were massacred in Amputuan, Maguindanao (a town located in the southern, primarily Muslim part of the country) when the vice mayor, "Toto" Mangudadatu, went to file a certificate of candidacy to run for governor of Maguindanao against political rival Andal Ampatuan Jr. (the Ampatuan clan had held a political stronghold over this province since 2001). As the convoy of journalists, friends, family, and political supporters approached the election office, they were greeted by over one hundred armed men, who began shooting at close range. Out of those killed, thirty-four were journalists, prompting the New York City–based watchdog group Committee to Protect Journalists to declare the Maguindanao massacre "the single deadliest event for the press since 1992, when CPJ began keeping detailed records on journalist deaths" (Committee to Protect Journalists 2009). More grisly were reports from the Department of Justice indicating that the female victims (approximately twenty, some pregnant) had been raped and then shot in the genitals before their bodies were dumped in mass graves (Agence France-Presse 2009).

With these events in mind, many human rights observers hoped that when Benigno Noynoy Aquino III was elected the fifteenth president of the Philippines on May 10, 2010, he would take swift measures to end the human rights crisis that had gripped the country since 2001. Instead, in mid-August, Aquino announced that he would *extend* the U.S.-backed counterinsurgency program Oplan Bantay Laya (Operation Freedom Watch) until January 2011, effectively continuing the policy of military aggression and state violence that has largely been responsible for the extrajudicial killings, kidnappings, and enforced disappearances of political activists throughout the nation. In a recent report assessing the first one hundred days of his presidency, human rights groups remained skeptical that Aquino would prove any different from Arroyo, noting that fourteen progressive activists had been killed since he took office (GMA News 2010). By remaining servile to the dictates of U.S. imperialist policy, Aquino continues down the well-worn path of Filipino presidents who have preceded him, ensuring the country will remain a maldeveloped, neocolonial formation.

At this critical juncture in Philippine history, I maintain that feminist scholarship needs to reorient itself to better grasp the totality of the crisis besetting America's former "pearl of the Orient." It is not clear that feminist theory, especially of the kind I have examined in previous chapters, will enable scholars to adequately comprehend both the repression of progressive activists and the collective resistance that such exploitation always generates. Within this context, Liza Maza's rousing demonstration of a nationalist, militant feminism, exemplified in the slogan MAKIBAKA! HUWAG MATAKOT! takes on a special significance. Indeed, the anti-imperialist nationalist feminist framework of the multisectoral Philippine women's movement is an exemplary model of a materialist brand of feminist theory and praxis. The movement's history of resistance against colonization, by both Spain and the United States, provides a much-needed alternative to the "textual activism" that characterizes the majority of contemporary feminist discourse.

BIBLIOGRAPHY

Adams, John. 2009. Filipina activists boost overseas workers. *Christian Science Monitor*, January 26.

Africa, Sonny. 2009. OFW remittances amid crisis: Govt's dependable source faces challenges. *IBON Features*, February 20.

Agence France-Presse. 2007. US military apologizes for South Korean rape case. *Philippine Daily Inquirer*, January 15.

———. 2009. Massacre women victims shot in genitals—DOJ chief. *Philippine Daily Inquirer*, November 27.

Aguilar, Delia D. 1981. Some thoughts on the oppression of women. In *Filipina insurgency*, by E. San Juan Jr., 171–181. Quezon City, Philippines: Giraffe Books.

———. 1988. *The feminist challenge: Initial working principles towards reconceptualizing the feminist movement in the Philippines*. Manila: Asian Social Institute in cooperation with the World Association for Christian Communication.

———. 1997. Gender, nation, and colonialism: Lessons from the Philippines. In *The women, gender, and development reader*, ed. Nalini Visvanthan, Lynn Duggan, Laurie Nisonoff, and Nan Wiegersma, 309–317. London: Zed Books.

———. 1998. *Toward a nationalist feminism*. Quezon City, Philippines: Giraffe Books.

Aguilar, Delia, and Karin Aguilar-San Juan. 2005. Feminism across our generations. In *Pinay power: Theorizing the Filipina/American experience*, ed. Melinda de Jesus, 167–183. New York: Routledge.

111

Agustin, Laura. 2007. *Sex at the margins: Migration, labour markets, and the rescue industry.* New York: Zed Books.

Ahmad, Aijaz. 1992. *In theory: Classes, nations, literatures.* New York: Verso.

Alarcon, Norma, Caren Kaplan, and Minoo Moallem. 1999. Introduction: Between woman and nation. In *Between woman and nation: Nationalisms, transnational feminisms, and the state,* ed. Caren Kaplan, Norma Alarcon, and Minoo Moallem, 1–18. Durham, NC: Duke University Press.

Alipala, Julie. 2007. Women's group presses review of RP-US military pact. *Philippine Daily Inquirer,* January 24.

Alston, Philip. 2007. Promotion and protection of all human rights, civil, political, economic, social, and cultural rights, including the right to development: Report of the special rapporteur on extrajudicial, summary, or arbitrary executions. New York: United Nations.

Anderson, Benedict. 1983. *Imagined communities: Reflections on the origins and spread of nationalism.* New York: Verso.

Anderson, Bridget. 2000. *Doing the dirty work?: The global politics of domestic labour.* London: Zed Books.

Angeles, Leonora C. 1989. Feminism and nationalism: The discourse on the woman question and the politics of the women's movement in the Philippines. M.A. thesis (unpublished), Department of Political Science, University of the Philippines, Quezon City.

———. 2003. Creating social spaces for transnational feminist advocacy: The Canadian International Development Agency, the national commission on the role of Filipino women, and Philippine NGOs. *Canadian Geographer* 47: 283–302.

Antrobus, Peggy. 2004. *The global women's movement: Issues and strategies for the new century.* London: Zed Books.

Arao, Danilo Arana. 2006. Supermaid solution proves permanence of OFW deployment. *Bulatlat,* August 6–12. http://bulatlat.com (accessed November 5, 2008).

Basch, Linda, Nina Schiller, and Cristina Blanc. 1993. *Nations unbound: Transnational projects, postcolonial predicaments, and deterritorialized nation-states.* New York: Routledge.

Bell, Laurie, ed. 1987. *Good girls/bad girls: Feminists and sex trade workers, face to face.* Toronto: Canadian Scholars Press.

Benhabib, Seyla. 1996. From identity politics to social feminism: A plea for the nineties. In *Radical democracy: Identity, citizenship, and the state,* ed. David Trend, 27–41. New York: Routledge.

Bernstein, Elizabeth. 2010. Militarized humanitarianism meets carceral feminism:

The politics of sex, rights, and freedom in contemporary anti-trafficking campaigns. *Signs* 36: 45–71.

Bhaba, Homi. 1994. *The location of culture*. New York: Routledge.

Blount, Roy Jr. 2008. Mark Twain: Our original superstar. *Time*, July 3.

Bonner, Raymond. 1988. *Waltzing with a dictator*. New York: Vintage.

Boyce, James K. 1993. *The Philippines: The political economy of growth and impoverishment in the Marcos era*. Honolulu: University of Hawaii Press.

Cabreza, Vincent. 2008. Thomasites root of RP-US friendship, says Kenneyon July 4. *Philippine Daily Inquirer*, July 6.

Castaneda, Dabet. 2007. 2 missing UP students tortured, raped inside military camp. *Bulatlat*, November 25–December 1. http://bulatlat.com (accessed October 14, 2008).

Chang, Grace. 2000. *Disposable domestics: Immigrant women workers in the global economy*. Boston: South End Press.

Chant, Sylvia, and Cathy McIlwaine. 1995. *Women of a lesser cost: Female labour, foreign exchange, and Philippine development*. London: Pluto Press.

Chossudovsky, Michel. 2003. *The globalization of poverty and the new world order*. Pincourt, QC: Global Research.

Choy, Catherine. 2003. *Empire of care: Nursing and migration in Filipino American history*. Durham, NC: Duke University Press.

Committee to Protect Journalists. 2009. Maguindanao death toll worst for press in recent history, November 25.

Constable, Nicole. 1997. *Maid to order in Hong Kong: An ethnography of Filipina workers*. Ithaca, NY: Cornell University Press.

———. 2003. *Romance on a global stage: Pen pals, virtual ethnography, and "mail-order" marriages*. Berkeley and Los Angeles: University of California Press.

Constantino, Renato. 1975. *The Philippines: A past revisited*, vol. 1. Quezon City, Philippines: Foundation for Nationalist Studies.

Cotter, Jennifer. 2001. Eclipsing exploitation: Transnational feminism, sex work, and the state. *Red Critique* (Spring). www.redcritique.org/spring2001/eclipsingexploitation.htm (accessed December 10, 2002).

Davis, Leonard. 1989. *Revolutionary struggle in the Philippines*. New York: St. Martin's Press.

de Guzman, Odine. 2003. Overseas Filipino workers, labor circulation in Southeast Asia, and the (mis)management of overseas migration programs. *Kyoto Review of Southeast Asia*, no. 3 (October). http://kyotoreview.cseas.kyoto-u.ac.jp/issue/issue3/article_281_p.html (accessed July 2, 2008).

de Jesus, Melinda. 2005. Introduction: Toward a peminist theory, or theorizing the Filipina/American experience. In *Pinay power: Theorizing the Filipina/American experience*, ed. Melinda de Jesus, 1–15. New York: Routledge.

del Callar, Michaela P. 2009. Illegal pinoys in Europe to be hit by EU policy. *Philippine Daily Tribune*, March 9.

Delacoste, Frederique, and Priscilla Alexander, eds. 1987. *Sex work: Writings by women in the sex industry.* San Francisco: Cleis Press.

Deleuze, Gilles, and Felix Guattari. 1983. *Anti-Oedipus: Capitalism and schizophrenia.* Minneapolis: University of Minnesota Press.

Delmendo, Sharon. 2004. *The star entangled banner: One hundred years of America in the Philippines.* New Brunswick, NJ: Rutgers University Press.

Ditmore, Melissa. 2005. Trafficking in lives: How ideology shapes policy. In *Trafficking and prostitution reconsidered: New perspectives on migration, sex work, and human rights*, ed. Kamala Kempadoo, with Jyoti Sanghera and Bandana Pattanaik, 107–126. Boulder, CO: Paradigm Publishers.

Docena, Herbert. 2006. On the job training: Are U.S. soldiers engaged in actual combat in the Philippines? *Asia Times*, March 9.

Doezema, Jo. 2010. *Sex slaves and discourse masters: The construction of trafficking.* New York: Zed Books.

Doty, Roxanne Lynn. 1996. *Imperial encounters: The politics of representation in north-south relations.* Minneapolis: University of Minnesota Press.

Dumlao, Doris. 2008. 23 million Filipinos living below Asia-Pacific poverty line. *Philippine Daily Inquirer*, August 27.

Ebert, Teresa L. 1996. *Ludic feminism and after: Postmodernism, desire, and labor in late capitalism.* Ann Arbor: University of Michigan Press.

———. 2009. *The task of cultural critique.* Urbana: University of Illinois Press.

Editorial: Absence of Violence. 2007. *Philippine Star.* www.abs-cbnnews.com .storypage.aspx?StoryId-79621 (accessed June 7, 2007).

Ehrenreich, Barbara, and Arlie Hochschild, eds. 2002. *Global woman: Nannies, maids, and sex workers in the new economy.* New York: Holt.

Eisenstein, Hester. 2009. *Feminism seduced: How global elites use women's labor and ideas to exploit the world.* Boulder, CO: Paradigm Publishers.

Enloe, Cynthia. 1990. *Bananas, beaches, and bases: Making feminist sense of international politics.* Berkeley and Los Angeles: University of California Press.

———. 2000. *Maneuvers: The international politics of militarizing women's lives.* Berkeley and Los Angeles: University of California Press.

Epstein, Barbara. 2001. What happened to the women's movement? *Monthly Review* (May): 1–14.

Eviota, Elizabeth. 1992. *The political economy of gender: Women and the sexual division of labour in the Philippines.* London: Zed Books.

Freedom from Debt Coalition. 2007. Debt snapshots. www.fdc.ph (accessed May 15, 2009).

GABRIELA. 1998. GABRIELA says no to VFA. Press release, http://members.tripod.com/~gabriela_p/6-pressreles/980213_vfa.html (accessed April 30, 2007).

GABRIELA Women's Party [GWP]. 2009. House probe on OFW 'Global Crisis Fund' urged. http://gabrielanews.wordpress.com/2009/01/19/ (accessed February 15, 2009).

Gibson, Katherine, Lisa Law, and Deirdre McKay. 2001. Beyond heroes and victims: Filipina contract migrants, economic activism, and class transformations. *International Feminist Journal of Politics* 3, no. 3: 365–386.

Gibson-Graham, J. K. 1996. *The end of capitalism (as we knew it): A feminist critique of political economy.* London: Blackwell.

Glodava, Mila, and Richard Onizuka. 1994. *Mail-order brides: Women for sale.* Fort Collins, CO: Alaken.

GMA News. 2009. Subic rape case: Major legal decisions. *GMA News*, February 11.

———. 2010. Aquino "forgives" 1st-100-days doomsayers. *GMA News*, October 2.

Gonzalez, Marcial. 2004. Postmodernism, historical materialism, and Chicano/a cultural studies. *Science and Society* 68: 161–186.

Grewal, Inderpal, and Caren Kaplan. 1994. Introduction: Transnational feminist practices and questions of postmodernity. In *Scattered hegemonies: Postmodernity and transnational feminist practices*, ed. Inderpal Grewal and Caren Kaplan, 1–33. Minneapolis: University of Minnesota Press.

Hardt, Michael, and Antonio Negri. 2000. *Empire.* Cambridge, MA: Harvard University Press.

Heng, Geraldine. 1997. "A great way to fly": Nationalism, the state, and the varieties of third-world feminism. In *Feminist genealogies, colonial legacies, democratic futures*, ed. M. Jacqui Alexander and Chandra Talpade Mohanty, 30–45. New York: Routledge.

Herr, Ranjoo Seodu. 2003. The possibility of nationalist feminism. *Hypatia* 18: 135–153.

Hilsdon, Anne-Marie. 1995. *Madonnas and martyrs: Militarism and violence in the Philippines.* Quezon City, Philippines: Ateneo de Manila University Press.

Hochschild, Arlie Russell. 2002. Love and gold. In *Global woman: Nannies, maids, and sex workers in the new economy*, ed. Barbara Ehrenreich and Arlie Russell Hochschild, 15–30. New York: Metropolitan Books.

Hoganson, Kristin L. 1998. *Fighting for American manhood: How gender politics provoked the Spanish-American and Philippine-American wars.* New Haven, CT: Yale University Press.

Hondagneu-Sotelo, Pierette. 1994. *Gendered transitions: Mexican experiences of immigration.* Berkeley and Los Angeles: University of California Press.

Hsia, Hsiao-Chuan. 2004. Internationalization of capital and the trade in Asian women: The case of "foreign brides" in Taiwan. In *Women and globalization,* ed. Delia D. Aguilar and Anne E. Lacsamana, 181–229. New York: Humanity Books.

IBON. 2010. RP jobs, quality of work in 2009 worst in 50 years. *IBON News,* March 16. www.ibon.org/ibon_articles.php?id=60 (accessed December 23, 2010).

Ignacio, Emily. 2005. *Building diaspora: Filipino community formation on the Internet.* New Brunswick, NJ: Rutgers University Press.

Jeffreys, Sheila. 2009. *The industrial vagina: The political economy of the global sex trade.* New York: Routledge.

Jimenez-David, Rina. 2009. At large: Confused about "Nicole." *Philippine Daily Inquirer,* March 20.

Kempadoo, Kamala. 1999. Slavery or work? Reconceptualizing third world prostitution. *Positions* 7, no. 1 (Spring): 225–237.

Kempadoo, Kamala, and Jo Doezema, eds. 1998. *Global sex workers: Rights, resistance, redefinition.* New York: Routledge.

Kempadoo, Kamala, ed., with Jyoti Sanghera and Bandana Pattanaik. 2005. *Trafficking and prostitution reconsidered: New perspectives on migration, sex work, and human rights.* Boulder, CO: Paradigm Publishers.

Kennedy, Elizabeth Lapovsky, and Agatha Beins. 2005. Introduction. In *Women's studies for the future: Foundations, interrogations, politics,* ed. Elizabeth Lapovsky Kennedy and Agatha Beins, 1–28. New Brunswick, NJ: Rutgers University Press.

Kirk, Gwyn, and Margo Okazawa-Rey. 1998. Making connections: Building an East Asia–U.S. women's network against U.S. militarism. In *The women and war reader,* ed. Lois Ann Lorentzen and Jennifer Turpin, 308–322. New York: New York University Press.

Kramer, Paul. 2006. *The blood of government: Race, empire, the United States, and the Philippines.* Chapel Hill: University of North Carolina Press.

———. 2008. The water cure: Debating torture and counterinsurgency—a century ago. *New Yorker,* February 25, 1–5.

Lacsamana, Anne E. 1998. Academic imperialism and the limits of postmodernist discourse: An examination of Nicole Constable's *Maid to Order in Hong Kong: Stories of Filipino Workers. Amerasia* 24, no. 3: 37–42.

————. 2004. Sex worker or prostituted woman?: An examination of the sex work debates in feminist theory. In *Women and globalization*, ed. Delia D. Aguilar and Anne E. Lacsamana, 387–403. New York: Humanity Books.

————. 2009. Identities, nation, and imperialism: Confronting empire in Filipina American feminist thought. In *Globalization and third world women: Exploitation, coping, and resistance*, ed. Ligaya Lindio-McGovern and Isidor Wallimann, 65–80. Surrey, UK: Ashgate.

Law, Lisa. 1997. Dancing on the bar: Sex, money, and the uneasy politics of third space. In *Geographies of resistance*, ed. Steve Pile and Michael Keith, 107–122. New York: Routledge.

Lee, Na Young. 2006. Gendered nationalism and otherization: Transnational prostitutes in South Korea. *Inter-Asia Cultural Studies* 7: 1–16.

Libang, Gert. 2007. Interview by author. Quezon City, Philippines, January 3.

Lichauco, Alejandro. 2005. *Hunger, corruption, and betrayal: A primer on U.S. neocolonialism and the Philippine crisis*. Manila: Citizens' Committee on the National Crisis.

Lyotard, Jean-Francois. 1979. *The postmodern condition: A report on knowledge*. Minneapolis: University of Minnesota Press.

MacInnis, Laura, and Stephanie Nebehay. 2007. Nordics top gender equity index, U.S. falls to 31st. *Reuters Alertnet*, November 7.

Magdoff, Harry, John Bellamy Foster, Robert W. McChesney, and Paul Sweezy. 2002. U.S. military bases and empire. *Monthly Review* (March): 1–14.

Mann, Susan Archer, and Douglas J. Huffman. 2005. The decentering of second-wave feminism and the rise of the third wave. *Science and Society* 69: 56–91.

Maragay, Dino. 2009. Nicole's recantation an "unfortunate" twist. *Philippine Star*, March 18.

McClintock, Anne. 1993. Family feuds: Gender, nationalism, and the family. *Feminist Review* 44: 61–80.

McKay, Susan. 1998. The psychology of societal reconstruction and peace: A gendered perspective. In *The women and war reader*, ed. Lois Ann Lorentzen and Jennifer Turpin, 348–362. New York: New York University Press.

Melo Commission Report. 2007. Independent mission to address media and activist killings, January 22.

Migrante International. Our history. http://migranteinternational.org (accessed December 27, 2010).

Mission for Migrant Workers. http://www.migrants.net (accessed February 2009).

Mondelo, D. L. 2007. Arroyo government "watchlist": Targeting progressive foreigners. *Bulatlat,* August 26–September 1. http://bulatlat.com (accessed September 8, 2007).

Moon, Katharine. 1997. *Sex among allies: Military prostitution in U.S.-Korea relations.* New York: Columbia University Press.

Murray, Alison. 1998. Debt bondage and trafficking: Don't believe the hype. In *Global sex workers: Rights, resistance, and redefinition,* ed. Kamala Kempadoo and Jo Doezema, 51–64. New York: Routledge.

Nagle, Jill, ed. 1997. *Whores and other feminists.* New York: Routledge.

Naiman, Joanne. 1996. Left feminism and the return to class. *Monthly Review* (June): 12–28.

National Commission on the Role of Filipino Women [NCRFW]. 2008. ASEAN lauds RP for closing the gender gap. Press release, January 28.

Nussbaum, Martha. 1999. The professor of parody. *New Republic* 220, no. 16 (February 22): 1–13.

Oliveros, Benjie. 2008. Disasters, disasters. *Bulatlat* 8, June 29–July 5. http://bulatlat.com (accessed July 3, 2008).

Ong, Aihwa. 1999. *Flexible citizenship: The cultural logics of transnationality.* Durham, NC: Duke University Press.

Orejas, Tonette. 2007. US marines promise no more rape in Luzon. *Philippine Daily Inquirer,* October 21.

Parrenas, Rhacel. 2001. *Servants of globalization: Women, migration, and domestic work.* Palo Alto, CA: Stanford University Press.

———. 2005. *Children of global migration: Transnational families and gendered woes.* Palo Alto, CA: Stanford University Press.

People's International Observers' Mission. 2007. A chicanery of elections: Initial findings and conclusion. *Samar News,* May. http://samarnews.com/news 2007/may/f1164.htm (accessed May 19, 2007).

Permanent People's Tribunal [PPT] Second Session on the Philippines. 2007. Verdict: Indicting the U.S.-backed Arroyo regime and its accomplices for human rights violations, economic plunder, and transgression of the Filipino people's sovereignty. http://philippinetribunal.org (accessed March 28, 2007).

Pheterson, Gail, ed. 1989. *A vindication of the rights of whores.* Seattle: Seal Press.

Pomeroy, William J. 1992. *The Philippines: Colonialism, collaboration, and resistance!* New York: International Publishers.

Quismundo, Tarra, and Julie Alipala. 2009. "Not Nicole's style," that's defense line. *Philippine Daily Inquirer,* March 19.

Regaldo, Connie. 2007. Interview by author. Quezon City, Philippines, January 4.

Republic of the Philippines. 1997. The anti-rape law of 1997. http://www

.unescap.org/esid/psis/population/database/poplaws/law_phi/phi_046 (accessed January 2007).

Revoir, Paul. 2008. Diplomatic storm over Harry Enfield's "slur on a nation" sketch of Filipina chased for sex. *Daily Mail*, October 8.

Richter, Linda. 1982. *Land reform and tourism development: Policy-making in the Philippines*. Cambridge, MA: Schenkman.

Roces, Mina. 2009. Prostitution, women's movements, and the victim narrative in the Philippines. *Women's Studies International Forum* 32: 270–280. doi: 10.1016/jwsif.2009.05.012 (accessed August 5, 2010).

Rodriguez, Robyn. 2008. Domestic debates: Constructions of gendered migration from the Philippines. *Scholar and Feminist Online*, no. 6.3 (Summer). www.barnard.edu/sfonline/immigration/print_rodriguez.htm (accessed January 28, 2009).

Rosca, Ninotchka. 2007. Rape case exposes U.S. domination of Philippine government. *Socialism and Liberation* 4, no. 3 (March 1). http://socialismandliberation.org/mag/index (accessed March 24, 2009).

Said, Edward. 1978. *Orientalism*. New York: Vintage Books.

San Juan Jr., E. 1998. *Filipina insurgency*. Quezon City, Philippines: Giraffe Books.

———. 2000. *After postcolonialism: Remapping Philippines–United States confrontations*. New York: Rowman and Littlefield.

———. 2005. Terrorism and revolution: The struggle for national democracy and socialism in the Philippines. *Cultural Logic: An Electronic Journal of Marxist Theory and Practice* 8. http://clogic.eserver.org/2005/sanjuan.html (accessed February 15, 2006).

———. 2007. *On the presence of Filipinos in the United States*. Salinas, CA: Sarimanok.

Santiago, Lilia Quindoza. 1995. Rebirthing Babayae: The women's movement in the Philippines. In *The challenge of local feminisms: Women's movements in global perspectives*, ed. Amrita Basu, 110–128. Boulder, CO: Westview Press.

Santos, Aida. 1984. Do women really hold up half the sky? Notes on the women's movement in the Philippines. *Diliman Review* 32: 1–12.

———. 1992. Gathering the dust: The bases issue in the Philippines. In *Let the good times roll: Prostitution and the U.S. military in Asia*, ed. Saundra Pollock Sturdevant and Brenda Stoltzfus, 32–44. New York: New Press.

Santos, Aida, Cecilia T. Hofmann, and Alma Bulawan. 1998. Prostitution and the bases: A continuing saga of exploitation. Coalition Against Trafficking in Women–Asia Pacific (Speeches/Papers), May.

Schirmer, Daniel B., and Stephen Shalom, eds. 1987. *The Philippines reader: A history of colonialism, neocolonialism, dictatorship, and resistance.* Boston: South End Press.

Stabile, Carol. 1997. Feminism and the ends of postmodernism. In *Materialist feminism: A reader in class, difference, and women's lives,* ed. Rosemary Hennessey and Chrys Ingraham, 395–408. New York: Routledge.

Stoler, Ann Laura. 1995. *Race and the education of desire: Foucault's history of sexuality and the colonial order of things.* Durham, NC: Duke University Press.

Sutton, Barbara, and Julie Novkov. 2008. Rethinking security, confronting inequality. In *Security disarmed: Critical perspectives on gender, race, and militarization,* ed. Barbara Sutton, Sandra Morgen, and Julie Novkov, 3–29. New Brunswick, NJ: Rutgers University Press.

Tadiar, Neferti. 2004. *Fantasy-production: Sexual economies and other Philippine consequences for the new world order.* Hong Kong: Hong Kong University Press.

Takaki, Ronald. 1989. *Strangers from a different shore: A history of Asian Americans.* New York: Back Bay Books.

Task Force Subic Rape. 2006. Briefing Paper: Rape and the VFA, 1–8. Manila: TSFR.

Torres, Tetch. 2006. U.S. Marine guilty of raping Filipina, 3 others acquitted. *Philippine Daily Inquirer,* December 4.

———. 2009. U.S. Marine in Subic rape case acquitted. *Philippine Daily Inquirer,* April 23.

Tulfo, Ramon. 2006. Comments on "Nicole" case. *Philippine Daily Inquirer,* December 21.

Uy, Veronica, and Joel Guinto. 2009. Palace: "VFA 2" not a secret. *Philippine Daily Inquirer,* February 20.

Vickers, Jeanne. 1994. *Women and the world economic crisis.* London: Zed Books.

Villapando, Venny. 1989. The business of selling mail-order brides. In *Making waves: An anthology of writings by and about Asian American women,* ed. Asian Women United of California, 318–327. Boston: Beacon Press.

Viola, Michael. 2007. Review: Building diaspora: Filipino community formation on the Internet. *Amerasia Journal* 33, no. 3: 161–164.

Visiting Forces Agreement. 1998. Agreement between the government of the Republic of the Philippines and the government of the United States of America regarding the treatment of United States Armed Forces Visiting the Philippines. http://www.vfacom.ph (accessed November 1, 2006).

Weekley, Kathleen. 2001. *The communist party of the Philippines 1968–1993.* Quezon City: University of Philippines Press.

West, Lois, and Lynn Kwiatkowski. 1997. Feminist struggles for feminist nationalism in the Philippines. In *Feminist nationalism,* ed. Lois West, 147–168. New York: Routledge.

Whitehead, Judith, Himani Bannerji, and Shahrzad Mojab. 2001. Introduction. In *Of property and propriety: The role of gender and class in imperialism and nationalism*, ed. Himani Bannerji, Shahrzad Mojab, and Judith Whitehead, 3–33. Toronto: University of Toronto Press.

Wiegman, Robyn. 2005. The possibility of women's studies. In *Women's studies for the future: Foundations, interrogations, politics*, ed. Elizabeth Lapovsky Kennedy and Agatha Beins, 40–60. New Brunswick, NJ: Rutgers University Press.

Wood, Ellen Meiksins. 1995. *Democracy against capitalism: Renewing historical materialism*. Cambridge, UK: Cambridge University Press.

Wright, Ann. 2008. Rape hobbles Bush administration policies. *Truthout*, May 26.

Zinn, Howard. 1980. *A people's history of the United States*. New York: Harper and Row.

INDEX

About the Author

Anne E. Lacsamana is Associate Professor of Women's Studies at Hamilton College. She is the coeditor of *Women and Globalization* (2004) and has published several articles on global/transnational feminist theory and U.S.-Philippine relations.